D1485172

WICCA
KITCHEN
WITCHERY

A Beginner's Guide to Magical Cooking, with Simple Spells and Recipes

BY LISA CHAMBERLAIN

Published by **Wicca Shorts**

ISBN: 1981138544

ISBN-13: 978-1981138548

Disclaimer

No part of this publication may be reproduced or transmitted in any form or by any means, mechanical or electronic, including photocopying or recording, or by any information storage and retrieval system, or transmitted by email without permission in writing from the publisher.

While all attempts have been made to verify the information provided in this publication, neither the author nor the publisher assumes any responsibility for errors, omissions, or contrary interpretations of the subject matter herein.

This book is for entertainment purposes only. The views expressed are those of the author alone, and should not be taken as expert instruction or commands. The reader is responsible for his or her own actions.

Adherence to all applicable laws and regulations, including international, federal, state, and local governing professional licensing, business practices, advertising, and all other aspects of doing business in the US, Canada, or any other jurisdiction is the sole responsibility of the purchaser or reader.

Neither the author nor the publisher assumes any responsibility or liability whatsoever on the behalf of the purchaser or reader of these materials.

Any perceived slight of any individual or organization is purely unintentional.

YOUR FREE GIFT

As a way of showing my appreciation for purchasing my book, I'm giving away an exclusive, free eBook to my readers—*Wicca: Little Book of Wiccan Spells*.

The book is ideal for any Wiccans who want to start practicing magic. It contains a collection of ten spells that I have deemed suitable for beginners.

You can download it by visiting:

www.wiccaliving.com/bonus

I hope you enjoy it.

CONTENTS

INTRODUCTION

Imagine, if you will, an old-fashioned rural cottage in the age before electricity. Candles light the cozy main room, where a woman tends a boiling cauldron over an open fire in the hearth. Jars of flour, sugar and other dry goods line the rustic wooden shelves above an oak-topped table, upon which several clay bowls filled with herbs are lined up to be ceremoniously emptied into the cauldron.

The brew may be a soup, a stew, a healing medicine, or a potion designed to bring about a specific magical outcome. It may even be some combination of these possibilities. After all, since all food originates within the sacred bounty of Mother Earth, anything that's edible has inherent magical potential, and the woman at the hearth knows this well.

In myths and folklore from virtually every culture around the world, food has been associated with magic, and some of these ancient traditions have survived into the 21st century. Probably the most well-known example is the blowing out of candles on a birthday cake.

The first such cakes were actually baked as offerings to Artemis, the Greek goddess of the Moon. They were moon-shaped and lit with candles in order to make them "shine" as the Moon does. Eventually, the cakes came to be used to celebrate birthdays, and it was an 18th century Germanic custom to number the candles on the cake according to the age of the celebrant, with an extra candle added in hopes that they would live another year.

These days, with life expectancy being considerably improved, the "birthday wish" one makes before blowing out the candles could be for anything, but this wish is usually kept secret. And though it may seem to most people to be simply a fun tradition, there's a kind of dramatic quality to this moment at a birthday gathering that suggests there's more belief in the power of wishing on a candle than the average person might admit.

The wishbone is another tradition with ancient roots, going back to the Etruscans, who used the breastbone of a goose to divine the weather. They would also rub the bone while making a wish. The Romans adapted this custom, using chickens, but due to its popularity, there often weren't enough "wishbones" to go around. Thus, the tradition of two people wishing on the same bone came into being. The bone would be snapped in two, and the holder of the longer piece would see their wish come true.

Another modern custom, the Halloween game of bobbing for apples, also comes from the Romans. As their culture merged with that of the Celts in the British Isles, the apples they brought with them came to feature in the Celtic festival of Samhain. The game was played by young single people, and the first to successfully bite into an apple would be the next to marry.

Although these few examples of ancient traditions have survived through the millennia, it's fair to say that for the most part, mainstream culture is more disconnected from the magic of food than it has ever been. This is because we are more separated from the sources of our food than we have ever been.

For the majority of human history, our ancestors spent much of their waking time actively hunting, growing and harvesting their sustenance, and therefore appreciating the role played by the Earth, the Sun, the Elements, etc. in the process.

These days, we can pull a packaged meal from the freezer, toss it in the microwave, press a few buttons, and have dinner on the table within minutes. Of course, there's a lot to be said for convenience on busy days, but what we gain in time saved is no comparison to what we lose in terms of nutrition, taste, and magical connection to the Earth and all she offers us.

Fortunately, there seems to be a resurgence of interest in many parts of the modern world in returning to a more direct connection to Nature when it comes to food—at least to some extent.

More and more people are growing at least some of their own herbs and vegetables themselves on family farms, in backyard gardens, and even on windowsills in urban environments. Organic food has become more popular and more accessible over the past few decades, as people wake up to the damage caused by industrialized agriculture to the planet and our health. At the same time, there has been an increasing interest in the more esoteric aspects of food and food production, leading many to discover the ancient practice now known as "kitchen witchery."

Also known as "kitchen magic," "pantry magic," "culinary wizardry" and other names, the art of intertwining food and magic is a natural pursuit for Wiccans, Witches and other Pagans who have an affinity for cooking. But the realm of kitchen witchery is also inhabited by people who don't practice magic in any other context, and who may not even consider themselves to be Witches or Pagans of any stripe.

These cooks simply work with an attitude of reverence for the Earth, intuiting the transformative energies of foods, and using what they have to create nourishing, magically powerful meals. They may also make medicines, teas, tinctures, candles and other kitchen crafts that all fall under the umbrella term of 'kitchen witchery."

This guide is designed for anyone who is interested in the magical potential of the seemingly ordinary work of preparing and cooking food. While written largely from a Wiccan perspective, most of the information within these pages is simply practical information, useful for anyone from any spiritual background—and any level of cooking ability—who would like to incorporate magical practices into their approach to eating.

Part One delves into the concept of kitchen witchery in the context of our ancient ancestors' relationship to food, and our modern esoteric understanding of the magical energies of the Earth's edible abundance. Part Two provides guidance for transforming your kitchen into a sacred space and offers examples of how you can approach the "mundane" act of cooking with a magical eye. Part Three is a mini-grimoire of sorts, with example recipes, rituals, and techniques for making the most out of the magical potential that various foods provide.

You don't have to be a master chef or a master magician to find useful information throughout these pages, but even if you are, this guide can still provide new ideas and fresh perspectives on the art of kitchen witchery. So roll up your sleeves and enjoy making magic in your kitchen!

Blessed Be.

WHAT IS KITCHEN WITCHERY?

THE ANCIENT HEARTH

It could be argued that the discovery of fire—how to create it and harness its power—was the beginning of full-fledged magical practice for our earliest ancestors. Not only did fire allow people to navigate the darkness of night and warm their modest dwellings in the cold months, but it also made it possible to transform previously inedible things like plant roots, stems, certain seeds and many animal parts into safe, digestible food.

This newfound ability surely must have seemed like a magical blessing from the unseen realms. In fact, the well-known Greek story of Prometheus, the god who takes a liking to human beings and decides to bring them the gift of fire, is just one of many ancient myths regarding fire's divine origins.

Of course, magic existed everywhere in the primordial world, in every aspect of nature—in the spirits of the land and water, the cycles of the Moon, cloud formations, weather patterns, and the behavior of animals and birds. Plants would almost certainly have had magical significance, as they made up the primary source of food, medicine and, eventually, shelter for these very early cultures. Indeed, the first "spell" ingredients would have been medicinal remedies from plant sources. That some plants could kill while others were sources of nourishment and healing was a testament to their formidable inherent power.

Yet fire also had a dual nature, one that was arguably more forceful. Able to cause rapid and widespread death and destruction, yet also enhance and sustain life, fire was the first medium through which plants, animals, trees, and even water could be completely transformed, for better or worse, right in front of one's eyes.

The fire over which food was cooked was therefore a very magical thing indeed. And as humans continued to evolve—discovering new food sources, developing new tools for cooking, and adapting their dwellings to accommodate indoor fire—this sacred place eventually became the hearth. It was the focal point of the home, where families gathered to warm themselves, dry wet clothes, bake bread, and cook meals.

As the central, sustaining element of daily life, the fire in the hearth was a living, breathing entity, governed by the deities of the hearth and treated with reverence and respect. This fire was a crucial part of the continuing evolution of what we now call "kitchen witchery."

Obviously, the hearth was not the only context for food-related spiritual practice. Rituals and magical beliefs accompanied every aspect of the acquisition and preparation of food. Ceremonies and offerings honored the deities of hunting and gathering, prayers were sent up for favorable weather and bountiful harvests, and gratitude was expressed to the animals and plants whose lives were taken in order for the people to live. Food was blessed before being consumed, both to offer thanks to the deities who ruled its provenance and to ask for protection from illness. This last practice has continued into modern times, in virtually all religions around the world.

The Earth, Sun and Moon were revered by the ancients for their roles in the cycles of life and death experienced by all living things, as were the countless solar, lunar, and terrestrial deities associated with abundance and sustenance. Actual food itself was also associated with the divine, as can be seen in the multitude of connections between gods and goddesses and specific foods.

For example, the Celtic god Lugh was associated with both the Sun and the wheat harvest. In ancient Greece, pomegranates were associated with several deities, including Persephone, Zeus and Dionysus. Foods connected to specific deities would be left out as offerings, as an act of gratitude as well as a prayer for such blessings to continue.

As ancient civilizations evolved, these traditions took root and were passed down from generation to generation, and traces of some of these practices are still present today. For example, many people throughout Europe still celebrate some version of the four Pagan festivals that marked the turning points of the agricultural year. The most well-known are those of the ancient Celts—Imbolc, Beltane, Lughnasa, and Samhain—but these holidays go by other names in other parts of Europe, such as Feast of Torches, May Day, Harvest Home, and Winter Nights.

Related to planting, harvesting, and animal husbandry, these festivals were all about the celebration of food in one way or another, with rituals, magic and feasting as the focal points of the holiday. These special days, along with the ancient solar festivals at the solstices and equinoxes, were later integrated into the Wheel of the Year as followed by Wiccans and many other contemporary Pagans.

In short, it's hard to see how contemporary magical practices could have existed without these ancient food-centered traditions leading the way. After all, it was the necessity of food that gave rise to the first spells, charms, blessings and even the origins of many deities. Food, in and of itself, was the impetus for the first magic. And though technology has evolved to the point where we don't need literal fire in order to cook our meals, whenever we stand over a piping hot stove we are still, ultimately, participating in the magic of the hearth.

THE KITCHEN WITCH

In many ways, the kitchen Witch of today is still attuned to the practices of the ancestors when it comes to food preparation.

These Witches may or may not grow their own food in gardens or on farms, or hunt or raise their own animals for consumption, but they do have an interest in and appreciation for the source of their sustenance. Food is treated with reverence for the magical phenomenon that it is, and all aspects of its preparation are approached as ritual, rather than as household "chores."

In this way, even the implements and gadgets involved in cooking—such as spoons, pots and pans, cheese graters, etc.—are considered magical tools. Practitioners of kitchen witchery will charge their ingredients with their own magical energy and focus their intention into every stage of the process when preparing food. They may create special dishes with specific magical intentions, or simply enhance everything they make with positive, divine energy.

Many kitchen Witches like to work "from scratch" as much as possible, avoiding processed and packaged foods in order to be closer to Mother Earth—the original source of all nourishment. But there are many different styles of kitchen witchery—as many as there are people who practice it—and no two paths are ever necessarily the same.

Generally speaking, kitchen witchery is a solitary path, and those who practice it may or may not also participate in a more "formal" path of magic such as those found in Wicca and other modern Pagan spiritual systems. In fact, many kitchen Witches do not practice other forms of magic, but keep their focus on the tangible world of the kitchen, where manifestation is always able to be experienced with the five senses and actually taken into the body.

They may incorporate specific rituals in their cooking, such as recipes and techniques handed down to them from generations past, or create herbal charms, medicines and teas for achieving particular goals, but they don't necessarily work with any deities or make distinctions between ritual tools and everyday kitchen tools. In fact, plenty of these practitioners may not even consider themselves to be Witches or magicians, seeing themselves simply as being in tune with the natural energies of the Earth's abundant gifts.

For those who do practice Wicca or another Pagan path, the kitchen may be viewed as an extension of their magical practice, and even as a place where the more ceremonial or symbolic aspects of magic find tactile, 3-dimensional applications. Here, the tools of ritual meet their practical counterparts: the chalice becomes a cup, the wand becomes a stirring spoon, the athame is now a chef's knife, and the cauldron is any pot with something simmering in it on a hot stove.

Recipes are spells, enacted not just in hope of magical manifestation but also for the purpose of enjoyable nourishment. Those who work with deity might devote some kitchen space to honoring relevant aspects of the Goddess and God, such as Cerridwen, a Celtic Mother goddess associated with grain, or Cernunnos, ancient god of the hunt.

Those whose practice emphasizes the Elements may focus on the roles that Earth, Air, Fire and Water play in the process of growing, preparing and eating food. And of course, Witches who celebrate the Sabbats love to prepare feasts for these special occasions, using seasonally appropriate foods such as poached eggs for Ostara/Spring Equinox and root vegetable stew for Samhain.

There is no correct or incorrect way to practice kitchen witchery—it is a truly eclectic form of magic that can be shaped according to your own knowledge, intuition and personal preferences. No special training or specific study is required. However, it can be very useful to have a working understanding of the inherent magical energy of food, especially for beginning kitchen Witches who are just embarking on their individual journeys.

Next, we'll explore a little bit of ancient mystical philosophy as it applies to the physical make-up of foods, and how the act of creating and eating specially prepared meals helps bring about the positive changes we seek in our lives.

FOOD AND MAGICAL ENERGY

As we've seen above, the concept of food as a magical manifestation is not new. In fact, it has been with us since the days of our earliest ancestors. But aside from the fact that food comes to us through the abundance of Mother Earth, and beyond the rather miraculous process of starting with mere seeds and ultimately ending up with dinner, just what is it that makes food so magical? And how does what we eat become a means of magic all by itself?

There are as many frameworks for viewing the inherent magical properties of food as there are belief systems in the world, but the Hindu concept of *prana* is an especially useful one for today's culinary magicians.

Prana is universal energy, viewed as an intelligent force running through all that is alive on Earth—humans, animals, trees and plants, and even some crystals—along with the air itself. When we eat, we take into our bodies the prana of the individual ingredients, and this energy merges into our personal prana.

In Chinese traditional culture, the equivalent of prana is called *chi*, which literally translates to "breath," and has been described by modern practitioners of Traditional Chinese Medicine as an energy field that runs through and around each living being. Interestingly, the Chinese writing for the word "chi" also has an implied meaning of "steam rising from rice as it cooks," which is a wonderfully appropriate image in the context of culinary magic!

Chi is actually known in various Asian cultures—as *ki* in Japan and as *khi* in Vietnam, for example—and many other cultures have a similar concept, such as the Hawaiian *mana*, and the Great Spirit found throughout the natural world in several Native American spiritual systems.

FOOD AS UNIVERSAL CONSCIOUSNESS

In Western mysticism, we find a few further concepts that can help broaden our understanding of this universal energy and the role it plays in the magical process, both in "regular" magic and in kitchen witchery.

For example, the Hermetic Principle of Mentalism, as found in the *Kybalion,* asserts that the Universe itself is one giant, interconnected mind. At its most basic level, all matter—both "living" and "nonliving"—is made up of information, or consciousness. All of creation is born out of consciousness, whether we're talking about human-made creations like automobiles and skyscrapers, or natural creations like mountains, rivers, animals and plants.

This consciousness is more evident in human beings and animals than in plants and inanimate objects, as the brains of living beings are directly interacting with everything around them (though plants also respond to their environments through sensory information).

But at the most fundamental level of the Universe, living beings are not separate or closed off from the inanimate world—all is consciousness, or, as the *Kybalion* states, "The All is Mind; the Universe is Mental." We can make a distinction between consciousness in thought form versus consciousness in material form, but the two interact with each other, as anyone who has worked a successful spell with any kind of magical tool can attest.

When it comes to prana or chi, these are viewed primarily as *living* energies, which fluctuate according to the exact physical makeup of a person, animal or plant. Hindu Ayurvedic philosophy is concerned with the quality of the prana in the food we eat—just how much life force is in any given meal? Likewise, Chinese medicine aims to raise or balance the level of a person's chi through adjustments to one's diet.

The implications for kitchen magic are that some foods have more potent universal energy—or consciousness—than others, and are therefore more likely to bring powerful results. In view of this particular framework, you'll find general guidelines below for choosing optimal ingredients for your magical culinary creations.

EATING AS TRANSFORMATION

Another Hermetic tenet that applies to kitchen witchery is the Principle of Correspondence. This is expressed in the Kybalion as "As above, so below; as below, so above," a phrase which has become part of many magical traditions.

In the classical model of this concept, "above" relates to the spiritual (or etheric) plane—the unseen level of reality that we don't perceive with our physical senses. "Below," then, is the material (or Earth) plane, where physical manifestations can be seen, touched, heard, etc. All creation begins as thought, or intention, which is sent out into the spiritual plane ("above"), made manifest, and then is brought into the material plane ("below").

These "planes" are essentially mirrors of each other, so that the change we seek happens at the very instant we visualize our magical request and send it out into the Universe. However, our human experience of linear time causes us to perceive the change as happening later, as it may take days, months, or even longer for the manifestation to become apparent in our lives.

We can see an example of this in the way the body interacts with the foods we eat. Whenever we make intentional choices about food—whether we're trying to lose weight, resolve a nutritional imbalance or cure an illness—it takes at least a little bit of time to see results. The change we're intending for has already happened "above," but it has to work its way through the physical body "below" before we can perceive it for ourselves. This is true of magical work involving food as well.

However, when we deliberately channel our personal energy into the food we eat (and the process of preparing it), we are likely to experience faster and more powerful results all around, as we have connected our conscious intent with the consciousness connecting the whole Universe.

Another way to explain the Principle of Correspondence is that what is true of the macrocosm (i.e., the entire Universe) is also true of the microcosm—or the Earth plane, where we experience our daily lives. This idea has been around in mystical circles since ancient times, and has parallels to a concept brought forth through modern quantum physics: at the most basic level, every particle of matter contains all others, because all matter in the Universe is fundamentally interconnected.

This can be a tough concept for the mind to integrate, as it truly runs counter to the way we perceive ordinary reality. After all, we see most things as being separate and distinct from one another, rather than "containing" each other.

However, the phenomena of digestion and metabolism of food in the body can serve as an enlightening example. You've probably heard the saying "you are what you eat," but have you ever stopped to think about how literally true that is? Every nutrient the body takes in and metabolizes becomes physically part of the body's cellular structure. For example, the baby spinach you added to your salad yesterday may now be fueling the cells in the bones of your fingers. The lentils in the soup you have for dinner tonight may become part of your liver tomorrow.

The body, as the "macrocosm," reflects the individual ingredients of every meal—or microcosm—that it absorbs and then transforms. When it comes to culinary magic, we take this transformational process to a whole new level—we are literally creating our bodies out of the conscious intentions we put into the food as we prepared it.

FOOD AND FREQUENCY

Because we literally are what we eat, whether or not we're actively working magic with our food, it's especially useful to keep in mind the Principle of Vibration. Just as all matter is made up of information, or consciousness, all matter is also constantly in motion, in the form of vibration.

Of course, as humans we can only perceive a particular range of vibrational frequencies, so we don't recognize solid, stationary objects as vibrating. Nonetheless, at the subatomic level, every particle of matter in every solid object is actually in motion. It is through this motion that the consciousness of the Universe moves, connecting all things together at the most basic level of reality.

The Principle of Vibration is important to kitchen witchery in two primary ways. First and foremost, it's essential to understand that just as physical matter has a vibrational frequency, so does nonphysical matter, including our thoughts and emotions. Our very consciousness, in other words, is vibration.

If we are experiencing negative thoughts and feelings, our vibrational frequency is lower than if we are in a happy mood and thinking positive thoughts. Witches who succeed in magic do so because they make sure the energy of their consciousness is at a sufficient vibrational frequency to effect the change they're seeking.

If you're trying your hand at a love spell but feeling lonely and sad as you work, you're not going to manifest a fulfilling romance. Likewise, a money spell worked with a vibrational frequency of fear of not having enough is unlikely to bring anything other than a continued lack of money.

This same concept applies to the preparation of food—whether or not you're actively working magic. Indeed, both Witches and non-Witches alike are susceptible to this basic universal principle of energy exchange. If you're angry or upset while you're making a soup, that energy will end up in the soup itself, and is likely to cause some kind of discomfort for those who eat it, whether on a physical or emotional level.

The next time you find yourself feeling heavy or unpleasant in any way after a meal, reflect on how it was prepared. Were you eating at a restaurant where the employees are unhappy? If you ate at home, what was the vibrational quality of your energy while you cooked? Furthermore, did you take time to appreciate your meal and savor each bite? Or did you wolf it down while watching TV or texting on your phone? Just as the vibrational frequency of the preparation of food is important, so is your personal frequency during the experience of eating the meal.

If you think of it in terms of spellwork, eating can be compared to the sealing of a spell. You don't allow your focused energy to dissipate before lighting the candle, speaking the words, or whatever other sealing action the spell calls for. When it comes to food magic—and, arguably, eating in general—you get the best results by keeping a high, focused vibration from start to finish.

The second reason the Principle of Vibration is important is that each ingredient in your magical meal also has its own vibrational frequency. Therefore, some foods are higher in vibration than others, contributing to a higher personal frequency as a result.

This is seen easily enough by comparing steamed vegetables and deep-fried vegetables. While the latter may be more appealing, depending on your personal preferences, the steamed version is definitely going to have a lighter impact on your digestion, resulting in a "cleaner," more high-frequency feeling after you eat.

This is because, as a cooking method, steaming allows the vegetables to preserve more of their prana (or chi), whereas deep frying reduces this energy. This doesn't mean that you can't make a magical creation out of fried food, but it may mean that more of your own personal focused intention is required to bring the meal closer to the vibrational frequency of the healthier food.

So if you're just starting out with your kitchen witchery practice, you may want to begin with simple recipes that call for fresh, healthy foods. This will allow you to really notice the energy of each ingredient you're working with, as well as observing your own vibrational frequency before, during, and after your magical meal.

Keep in mind, however, that the quality of your focused intention is still the most important factor in any kind of magic. This makes it important to work with foods you truly enjoy. If you don't actually like the meal you're making, you're unlikely to summon the vibrational frequency needed to reach your magical goal while preparing and eating it.

OPTIMAL FOODS FOR A MAGICAL DIET

As any experienced Witch will tell you, your own personal energy and ability to focus that energy into your intention is the most important factor when it comes to any kind of magic, including kitchen magic. So again, when you're literally cooking up a spell, it makes sense to work with food you truly love. That being said, if you want to make the most out of the abundant gifts that Mother Nature has made available to you in your magical work, there are a few guidelines well worth keeping in mind.

Because different foods have differing amounts of prana, or chi, choosing foods with the highest available quality of energy is ideal. We have seen that the vibrational frequency of any given meal affects us physically, mentally and emotionally. This frequency is determined not just by the energy of the people involved in preparing the meal, but also by the ways in which the food is grown, harvested and processed before you bring it into your kitchen.

The quality of the prana—the life force—in each ingredient has a direct correlation to the vibrational frequency of the meal as a whole. This life force is at its most vital in foods that have not undergone any processing before they are eaten. The more processing that takes place, the more prana is diminished. So fresh, whole foods that have been harvested very recently are the ideal ingredients—not just for magical cooking, but for your own personal vitality as well.

For example, a ripe tomato still attached to its vine is at its optimal state of living energy. As soon as it is picked, this energy begins to wane, as the tomato has been severed from its life-giving source. Of course, there is still plenty of prana within the tomato, allowing it to continue ripening on the shelf until it is eaten—either by you or by fruit flies and/or invisible bacteria that will ultimately cause it to rot if it remains there.

People who love tomatoes will often simply cut these ripe, fresh beauties into slices and eat them raw, perhaps seasoned with a little salt and pepper. The deliciousness of this experience is due in large part to the high level of prana—and therefore the high vibrational frequency—of the tomato at this stage. Furthermore, the content of certain nutrients, such as vitamin C, is higher in the tomato's raw state than once you've cooked it, as heat further reduces the life force of any food.

Of course, this doesn't mean fruits and vegetables should only ever be eaten raw—in fact, there are other nutritional and digestive benefits of many foods that only become available through the cooking process. Indeed, the nutritional aspects of raw versus cooked foods are incredibly complex, and are not necessarily important to consider from a magical framework. And given that kitchen witchery is all about the transformation of ingredients into a magical creation, the action of cooking is very often an integral step.

The point is that whether your food is raw or cooked, "fresh is best" in terms of vibrational frequency. The tomato you pluck from your garden or pick up at your local farmer's market is far more alive and potent than a tomato that spent a week on a truck, being driven hundreds or thousands of miles from its origin to your grocery store, losing more and more of its prana each day.

The fresh tomato is also higher in frequency than one that has been canned, no matter how fresh it was at the time of the canning process. The same is true for frozen vegetables and fruits—while they may still be of very high quality, they do lose vitality in the process of being frozen and then thawed.

Of course, it can be extremely difficult, if not impossible, to cook all of your meals without relying on any canned or frozen ingredients whatsoever—especially during the winter. So don't let a lack of availability of fresh foods stop you from creating the magical meal you're wanting to make. Just do your best to include as many fresh ingredients as possible, and look for high-quality canned and frozen produce when these items are necessary.

One way to maximize your use of fresh, locally available food is to eat with the seasons. If you follow a Wiccan or other Pagan path, you already do this to some extent at the Sabbats, as the feasts for these occasions always feature foods of the seasons in which they occur. But you needn't limit yourself to Sabbat celebrations when it comes to eating according to the Wheel of the Year. Instead, you can use the Wheel as a guide to magical menu planning throughout each season.

For example, the celebration of Lammas, or Lughnasa, usually emphasizes summer squash and corn, among other foods. During the weeks of July through the end of August, or whenever squash and corn are locally available, you might try working food magic for enhancing your spiritual awareness, a magical goal associated with both. This is a great way of harmonizing your magic with the energies of the season, as well as working with the powers of the Earth in your own particular part of the globe.

In addition to freshness, another factor to consider is the methods by which the food you purchase has been grown. Over the past few decades, conventional, large-scale agriculture has come under increasing scrutiny when it comes to the use of pesticides and genetically modified organisms, as well as soil degradation due to monoculture farming, chemical runoff from fields into our water supply, and other practices that seem to be impacting both humans and the Earth in alarming ways.

The "big agro" corporations (as they are often called in the U.S.) would appear to be driven entirely by profit, rather than by providing safe, nutritious food to the populations they serve. The corporate greed and widespread environmental damage associated with conventional agriculture is certainly at odds with the ethos of Wicca and other Pagan paths.

Even more to the point, however, the food produced by these methods is lower in prana, and therefore lower in vibrational frequency, than food produced in harmonious balance with the Earth. These days, more and more people are turning to organic produce, which as a result has become more widely available and more affordable than it was several years ago. Though still more expensive than conventionally grown produce, organic food is almost always of better quality and taste, and is grown in a way that honors the natural processes of the life cycle on Earth.

This makes it a better choice not only for culinary magic, but for everyday eating in general. If budget concerns have kept you from buying organic foods, consider making a compromise by buying at least one or two organic items the next time you go shopping. You can do research online for the foods that have been found to contain the highest amounts of pesticides and other contaminants, and switch to organics for at least those items. The Earth will thank you, as will your body and your magic!

While your magical potential is ultimately only as limited as your imagination, there are some foods that are truly just not suited for kitchen witchery. Packaged and frozen meals, for example, don't really offer any opportunity for you to create anything—you simply pop them in the oven or into a pot on the stove and heat them up. In addition, the life force in these foods is greatly reduced by the amount of processing they've been through (again, no matter how high quality the ingredients might be).

If you're in a pinch, you can add a little of your own magical energy to such meals by charging some fresh herbs to spruce up the pre-cooked food, or putting together a quick salad to accompany it. By and large, however, any spellwork involving food should use fresh, whole ingredients as much as possible.

THE VEGETARIAN QUESTION

You may have noticed that the discussion in this guide thus far has been focused on plant-based foods—fruits, vegetables and grains—rather than on animal-derived foods. This is because the vibrational frequency of plant foods is, on the whole, much higher than that of meat, fish, poultry, etc.

This may seem counter-intuitive, since the level of universal consciousness within animals would seem to be higher than that within plants. However, the quality of the prana in animal-derived foods is greatly reduced by the manner in which animals are raised for consumption in the 21st century, particularly within the United States.

Most of the animals we eat have lived their entire lives in tightly enclosed, often dark and very crowded spaces, which is counter to the way a living, breathing, conscious being is meant to spend its life. Many are fed or injected with hormones and antibiotics designed to maximize profits for the meat industry, resulting in food that is not really "natural" at all. These practices diminish the life force within the meat that is produced, making it less efficient for magical purposes.

Furthermore, the environmental pollution that results from the heavily industrialized production (raising, slaughtering and processing) of meat is not conducive to a harmonious relationship with the Earth. This includes many fish farms, as well as commercial wild-caught fish, which are quickly being depleted from our oceans around the world. These issues can be problematic for those Wiccans and other Witches who choose to work magic under the ethos of "harm none," since there is arguably a vibration of "harm" present in the energy of industrialized meat.

This information is not intended to be an argument for vegetarianism. What you eat is absolutely your own decision! Nonetheless, this guide will focus on kitchen witchery of the vegetarian kind, due to the vibrational issues outlined above, and in the interest of being accessible to all readers.

Of course, this doesn't mean you can't work magic with meat—in fact, there are magical cookbooks available that include meat in their recipes, and it is not uncommon for meat to be present at Sabbat feasts. As with any other form of magic, you should feel free to develop your own individual practice, and to work with the foods you enjoy, no matter where they are sourced from.

On that note, it's worth mentioning that there are alternatives to "big agriculture" when it comes to meat consumption. There has been an increase in small, family-run farms where animals are treated with far more care and respect than those in the settings described above. Many of these farms are organic, and the meat they produce is on the whole healthier, higher in life force energy, and far less destructive to the environment. You may want to take a look around your area for local family farms, or ask at your local grocery store for more humane and environmentally sustainable options.

Finally, if you hunt your own game or go fishing in wild streams and lakes, you will have a much stronger, more personal energetic connection to the animal(s) you bring home and the food you derive from them, just as our ancestors did. Working with food you caught yourself would arguably be the most potent choice available when it comes to meat and magic, as it gives you an opportunity to directly honor and give thanks to the spirit of the animal whose life you took.

This was an integral part of indigenous peoples' approach to eating meat, as the animals were generally respected as living beings in their own right. Just try to be cognizant of ecological sustainability—hunt during legal seasons and don't take more than you need.

FURTHER CONSIDERATIONS

When it comes to maximizing your mastery of the magical energy of food, a few more tips are worth mentioning here.

First, understand that the methods you use in your cooking are as important as the ingredients themselves. The more hands-on, the better, as this is how you combine your personal energy with the energy of the ingredients you're working with. For example, if you're making a stir fry, opt for slicing and dicing fresh vegetables yourself, rather than buying a pre-sliced frozen veggie mix. Try making your own soup stocks rather than purchasing pre-made stocks.

Of course, most people don't have all day long to make complex from-scratch meals, so make whatever concessions you need to in order to accommodate your personal circumstances. But as you begin to think of cooking as magical work, you may just find yourself making more time for doing things "the old-fashioned way."

One "rule" that is definitely recommended is to avoid using a microwave for any aspect of magical cooking. Although these devices have come a long way over the past few decades and are generally not considered to be unsafe for our health as they once were, they still heat via radiation, which is not exactly compatible with the life force energy of the foods themselves.

If you're not convinced of this, try making a microwaved meal and a stove-cooked meal (of the same type of food) together and see which one tastes more "alive." Even when it comes to water, electric or gas heating is preferable to radiation. So if you've been in the habit of microwaving water for magical teas, consider getting an electric or stove-top tea kettle instead.

Finally, as a general practice, avoid wasting food as much as you can. Just as you wouldn't simply throw out leftover magical herbs, crystals, or other supplies, you want to honor the energy of your food by putting it to positive use. When it comes to perishable foods, buy only what you need. (For help with this, avoid grocery shopping on an empty stomach!)

When planning menus, prioritize using up fresh food first, rather than leaving it to go bad in the refrigerator. Freeze leftovers or eat them the next day to take maximum advantage of their taste and nutritional value. And if you can, compost your food scraps, as this is a great way to thank the Earth for her abundance and to participate directly in the life cycle of the soil.

BEING PRACTICAL

Hopefully, you now have a clearer sense of how food itself facilitates magical transformation, as well as how to approach choosing ideal ingredients for kitchen witchery. However, don't feel that you absolutely must grow your own food or buy only organic, local produce in order to work successful culinary magic.

While using fresh, healthy, prana-filled foods is always ideal, the single most important factor when it comes to kitchen magic is your personal energy—your vibrational frequency and ability to focus your intention. So there's no need to completely overhaul your diet overnight. To do so would likely be more disorienting than useful when it comes to being centered in your personal power.

Instead, start with foods you know you enjoy, and are comfortable preparing. If your go-to staples have always been of the canned or frozen variety, then by all means use them in your first forays into magical cooking. But make it a goal to gradually "upgrade" to fresher, more vibrant versions of these ingredients as you grow in your practice.

As you make this transformation, you will see the benefits—not only in terms of physical well-being, but on the magical level as well.

KITCHEN MAGIC FOR THE CULINARILY CHALLENGED

Generally speaking, most people would probably assume that those who practice magic—particularly any forms involving herbs and other natural ingredients—are at least decent hands in the kitchen, if not adept cooks.

This would certainly have been true for our ancestors, who would have at least had to know how to put a basic meal together, lest the family starve. Today, however, it is possible (and even common) to get by in life on microwaved food and take-out, so cooking has become much more optional.

If you're a Witch whose culinary skills don't go much beyond operating a can opener or slapping together a peanut butter and jelly sandwich, you might find the idea of kitchen witchery rather daunting. But don't be discouraged by any lack of experience. After all, even the most talented of chefs had to start from the beginning!

First of all, you *can* work kitchen magic with a can of beans or a simple sandwich. As with any other type of magic, the focus on your intention is far more significant than the specific objects you're working with. Often, the simplest spells have the biggest impact, as the lack of complicated ingredients and instructions makes it easier for the spell-caster to focus on their intention.

The same can be said for kitchen magic. In fact, one of the most commonly used forms of kitchen witchery—magical teas—is about as simple as it gets. As long as you can boil water, you can work a magical tea spell! So don't ever think you need to be a fancy cook in order to take advantage of the magic of food.

That being said, learning to cook from scratch is very much worth the effort, whether or not you're pursuing a kitchen witchery practice. As you learn to prepare your own food, you will feel more empowered to create change in your own life, and experience improved energy on the physical, emotional and spiritual levels. You'll also be deepening your relationship with the Earth, and therefore, your magic, no matter what form it takes!

The best way to approach learning to cook is to start simply. There are many cookbooks out there for beginners, featuring recipes with manageable steps and ingredients. And the internet is chock full of easy-to-find instructions for any question you might have. So start by finding some recipes that appeal to you—what sounds good to eat?

You don't even need to try cooking for specific magical purposes just yet. Instead, you might just focus on building a modest repertoire of meals you'll enjoy making repeatedly. In fact, if you pay attention to synchronicity, you may find that the food that appeals to you as you browse recipes is already associated with a magical goal or life improvement that would benefit you at this time.

Finally, allow yourself time to learn. Just as you can't become a magical adept in a matter of weeks, you're not going to be whipping out three-course meals right out of the gate.

When you're learning a new recipe or cooking technique, try it out at least once before incorporating a specific magical intention into it. You need focus and confidence to successfully send out your intention to the Universe, so save the culinary spellwork for foods you can prepare without needing to pay attention to complex recipe instructions. Again, this doesn't mean that you should hold off on trying out kitchen magic until you've gotten the hang of actual cooking. While you're getting your culinary education, you can still practice kitchen witchery with meals you already know how to make.

ETHICS OF MAGICAL COOKING

Before we move on to the more practical sections of this guide, it's important to take a moment to examine the potential implications of working kitchen magic, especially when it comes to cooking for other people. After all, you can choose the most prana-filled, high-vibrational foods in the world and create the most intention-filled, magically-focused meal you've ever made in your life, but if your motives aren't cleanly aligned with positive magic, you might be going to a whole lot of trouble just to end up with a whole lot of trouble!

When it comes to spellwork, the Wiccan philosophy states "harm none." On its face, this statement is self-explanatory, but it's important to note that "harm" also includes any form of manipulation attempted through magical means, no matter how innocent or benevolent the Witch's intentions may be.

This means that we don't attempt to lure a potential romantic partner with an aphrodisiac appetizer, or get our boss to give us a raise by bringing them magically charged doughnuts. It also means we don't serve magical meals "on the sly" to friends and family members, even if the spell we used in the process is for excellent physical health or other positive intentions. Just as we don't work candle spells or make charmed herbal sachets for others without their permission, we don't do magical cooking without it, either.

Since we're dealing with food rather than other kinds of magical work, however, some ethical aspects of kitchen witchery can be a bit less cut and dried. For example, a mother of young children who have come down with the flu could certainly be in the right for adding extra healing magic to a brothy soup.

It's a different thing, however, for a parent to use magical food on a teenager in an effort to get him to clean his room, as this is interfering with free will. Of course, interfering with free will is often part of parenting, but when it comes to changing a child's behavior, the effort should come through communication, boundaries and discipline rather than manipulative magic.

What if you're attending a potluck and want to charge up your contribution of pasta salad with vibrations of merriment for the occasion? In this situation, you just need to be clear and careful about your intention as you prepare the food. By all means, put your positive, joyful energies into each step of the process, but don't visualize the food itself *causing* the other people to be happy and have a good time.

Remember that it's enough to simply put your love into the food you offer to others, and that if you do so, they will always benefit from what you serve them. Anyone with a grandmother who baked the best pie on the planet or had the world's best chicken soup recipe will understand this basic truth: food created lovingly for others is its own magic—no spellwork required.

PUTTING IT ALL TOGETHER

So far, we've examined the roots of modern kitchen witchery, its ties with Wicca and other Pagan practices, and some of the esoteric theory behind the magical energy of food. Hopefully, those who are new to cooking in general have also gained some confidence about trying kitchen witchery, and inspiration for choosing magically potent, prana-rich foods to incorporate into their practice.

In Part Two, we'll explore many practical suggestions for turning your kitchen into a sacred space and beginning to think like a magician in the culinary arena. And we'll take an in-depth look at one example of how you can apply what you've learned about the energy of food to the creation of a single, simple dish: magical marinara sauce. By the end of this next section, you'll be ready to start practicing kitchen magic on your own, even before you get to the kitchen grimoire in Part Three!

SECTION TWO

THE WITCH'S KITCHEN

THE KITCHEN AS YOUR ALTAR

As we saw in Part One, our ancestors made the hearth the focal point of their homes, a place where food was cooked and shared among family members and friends.

These days, an actual hearth is seen as something of a luxury, rather than a standard feature of a home, and those lucky enough to have a working fireplace don't tend to cook much over the flames. Instead, modern technology has moved the preparation of food entirely to the kitchen, and depending on the layout of the home, this may be where meals are eaten, as well. In a sense, the oven and stove top now serve as the hearth, metaphorically standing in for the sacred fire that once warmed everything—and everyone—in the home.

Viewed in this light, the kitchen as a whole can be thought of as a kind of altar, where sacred gifts from the abundant Earth are transformed into new creations that nourish and benefit the body. For the kitchen Witch, this metaphor becomes quite literal, as magical techniques are merged with culinary skills to manifest not just nourishing meals, but desired changes in one's reality. Of course, there's a significant difference between a kitchen and an altar you might keep for your ritual and/or magical practice: the kitchen serves many mundane purposes, while the altar is kept strictly for spiritual activities.

Depending on your living situation and your personal practice, you may or may not be able to treat your kitchen as an altar on an "all day, every day" basis. After all, it's not exactly easy to maintain a magical state of mind when you're rushing to make a quick breakfast before dashing out the door in the morning. Nonetheless, if you want to develop a successful kitchen witchery practice, it's beneficial to begin thinking of your kitchen as a sacred space—one in which magic can be worked at any time, for any purpose.

Below, you'll find many suggestions for transforming your kitchen into a sacred space—a room-sized altar—no matter its size or current condition, and no matter whom you might be sharing it with. Creating your own Witch's kitchen will likely take a fair amount of work at the outset, but the effort will be well worth the magical experiences to come!

THE IMPORTANCE OF ENCHANTING YOUR KITCHEN

The Hermetic Principle of Vibration tells us that the subtle energetic aspects of preparing and eating food cannot be ignored if you want your kitchen witchery practice to be successful. The most crucial player when it comes to these energies is the person preparing the meal, as any negative emotions that are active within the cook are bound to end up in the food. Therefore, it's important to make sure you're in a positive mood when working your culinary magic, no matter what.

While this may seem like a tall order after a long, stressful day at work, it's usually not too difficult to transform your vibrational frequency if you're willing to let go of your less-than-pleasant state of mind. Treat yourself to a brief meditation session before you get started, smudge yourself with sage, or take a cleansing bath or shower if you have time. When it's time to cook, play music that puts you in a good mood, and allow yourself to enjoy anticipating the delicious meal you're now preparing.

Setting the intention to have a positive experience in the kitchen is an excellent habit to get into, as your positive energy will contribute to more consistently enjoyable and successful cooking, whether you're preparing a magical meal, cooking for a Sabbat celebration, or simply making an ordinary breakfast.

There may be situations, however, where no matter how enthusiastic you are going in, your kitchen mojo just isn't where you'd like it to be. Perhaps you keep burning your pasta sauces, or can't get the rice to turn out right no matter how carefully you measure the water. Maybe you keep dropping your stirring spoons on the floor, turning on the wrong burners on the stove top, or setting off the smoke alarm just by making toast.

If you've ever had a run of bad luck in the cooking department, you're definitely not alone. Many Witches (and many more non-magical types) have experienced what amounts to a "kitchen jinx" at one point or another. Whether it's that your meals just aren't tasting as good as you know they could, or you're literally starting fires every time you try to cook, it's quite possible that the problem isn't your personal energy, but rather the energy of your kitchen.

ADDRESSING ENERGETIC IMBALANCES

Right now, if you can, go take a good look at your kitchen. (If you're not at home, close your eyes for a moment and visualize your kitchen as it looked when you last saw it.) As you stand in the center of this space, whether physically or in your mind's eye, how does your body feel?

Take a moment to check for any feelings of constriction or any other negative sensations. Now check in with your emotional state. Is there any anxiety, sadness, or frustration coming up for you?

If so, you're almost certainly picking up on an energetic imbalance within the physical space of your kitchen. And even if you're not noticing any particular sensations, it's still quite possible that your kitchen is in a less-than-ideal energetic state, especially if you've been plagued with any of the bad luck described above. But there's no need to worry, as you can clear out any pesky "kitchen jinx" or other unpleasant energy with a good cleaning—on both the physical and ethereal levels.

As any sensitive Witch knows, physical spaces are repositories of non-physical energy. This means that thoughts, moods, emotions, and energetic imprints of past events can linger within the walls of any space that isn't energetically cleared on a fairly regular basis. In other words, you don't have to live in a "haunted" house to have a kitchen in need of rebalancing.

In fact, any kitchen that hasn't been in use specifically as a "magical" kitchen before is almost certainly going to need an energetic overhaul before your practice can truly take off. This is especially true if you live in an apartment or house that has been rented by many different tenants over the years.

Does this mean you have to scrub your entire kitchen down from top to bottom? Well, if you want to maximize the magical potential of your kitchen witchery practice, then the answer is yes. But if you aren't able to dive right into a deep-clean before you cook your next meal, there are smaller, less intensive methods for temporarily addressing energetic imbalances:

Declutter

Straightening up countertops, tables and any other visible surfaces in your kitchen helps ease any underlying sense of chaos or disorder that you may not even realize is bothering you. This is basic Feng Shui 101, and is applicable to any room in your home, but it's a very effective practice in the kitchen, and should ideally be done on a daily basis, especially just before you begin preparing a meal.

Sweep

Another practice to keep up daily if possible, sweeping the kitchen floor with a broom keeps energy from stagnating in corners and discourages Nature's little critters from venturing in to see what's for dinner. The broom is, of course, a signature symbol of the Witch, and its power to transform energy on a subtle level should never be underestimated.

If it's feasible, keep a broom specifically for your kitchen. This isn't strictly necessary, but it's nice to avoid mixing energies with any other rooms you sweep in your house. If you have a ritual broom or besom, you can also "sweep" your kitchen as an additional step, just as you would the sacred space where you hold magical rituals. (Of course, this doesn't mean actual sweeping—never let your ritual broom touch the kitchen floor!)

Smudge

Burning sage, lavender, rosemary, or a combination of these purifying herbs in a smudge stick will clear out leftover, unwanted energy from any space. If your kitchen feels particularly negative, however, you might want to try burning palo santo, which works more specifically on darker energies. All smudging is more effective when the space has been cleaned, so do at least wipe down counters and sweep the floor before taking this step.

Leave a window or door open for the unwanted energy to escape through. If you're dealing with really tough negative energy, you may want to smudge daily for at least seven days to make a lasting impact. However, you'll still need to do a thorough deep clean of the kitchen in order to make a permanent improvement.

MAGICAL FOOD STARTS WITH A CLEAN KITCHEN

It's often said that truly good cooking requires making a mess. This may indeed be the case, depending on your style and approach to culinary creations, but *beginning* the process with a clean kitchen is always recommended. In other words, clean up the old mess before you make a new one.

Just as you wouldn't begin a new Sabbat or Esbat ritual without having cleared away any remnants of the prior ritual (on both the physical and ethereal levels), you don't want to start making a magical dinner while last night's dishes are still sitting dirty in the sink. So get in the habit, if you aren't already, of beginning your kitchen work with a "clean slate." You will find you get better results, especially when whatever you're creating is really important to you.

Taking this philosophy further, it really does benefit you to do a thorough, detail-oriented deep clean of your entire kitchen at least once a year. This means cleaning the inside and outside of your refrigerator, freezer, cupboards, microwave, any other frequently used appliances (such as blenders and coffee makers) and yes, of course, your oven. You'll also need to clean under and behind everything that can be moved (including the oven and refrigerator) as well as all furniture, windows, and even walls—especially if they're painted and collect dust or grease over time.

If this sounds overwhelming, know that you don't have to do it all at once. Take it in stages, focusing on one area or appliance at a time. But do try to get it done within a few days, in order to really feel the benefits of the entire kitchen being sparkling clean all at once.

This is a perfect project to take on in preparation for the Sabbat of Imbolc (Feb 2 in the Northern Hemisphere, Aug 2 in the Southern Hemisphere), the traditional time when our ancestors would begin purifying their homes after being shut in over the long winter. But if Imbolc is a long way away, you certainly don't have to wait—feel free to start your kitchen deep clean today!

When it comes to cleaning supplies, be sure to show as much care and respect for the Earth as you can. Use all-natural cleaners whenever possible, and try to favor reusable cloths over paper towels. Avoid harsh chemical cleaners, as these are harmful both to people and the environment.

If you're dealing with an old, neglected oven with a ton of grime, you may need to make an exception, as all-natural products don't always get the toughest jobs done. As a general rule, however, remember that your kitchen is essentially an altar in and of itself, so unless they're absolutely necessary, chemicals and pollutants have no place there.

You can actually make your own cleaning products with essential oils, vinegars, baking soda and other natural ingredients, which you can then magically charge with specific intentions, if you like. Plenty of DIY cleaning recipes are available with a bit of research, and you'll find a couple of examples in Part 3 of this guide.

So when you're ready to completely overhaul the energy of your kitchen, put on some good music and make it as enjoyable as possible. As you sweep, wipe and scrub away old dirt and grime, understand that you are also clearing out unwanted energy from your life. By giving this level of attention to your kitchen, you're making room for all kinds of goodness and joy—not just in terms of food, but also prosperity, love, health, and anything else you want to manifest in your life.

Mop the floor last, and then when all is dry and sparkling clean, give the whole kitchen a good smudge with one or more of the herbs mentioned above. You can then follow up by burning sweet grass or cedar to welcome new, harmonious and loving vibrations into your newly enchanted kitchen.

KITCHEN ALTARS AND MAGICAL DECORATING

As discussed above, the kitchen can be seen as an altar in and of itself. However, given that plenty of mundane activities take place in this area of the home, it can be very effective to create a focal point for the specifically magical aspects of life in the kitchen.

A kitchen altar serves this purpose brilliantly. Here, you can keep any items that resonate with your kitchen witchery practice. This may include representations of the Goddess and God, such as candles, small statues, paintings, or other imagery. A small cauldron is an ideal symbol for a kitchen altar, as well as an athame and/or a chalice. You might also choose particular runes, hieroglyphs, or symbols from other esoteric systems that represent qualities you wish to attract to your kitchen practice, such as health, abundance, or success.

Depending on how much room you have, you might include a small potted plant or two. Edible herbs are a particularly appropriate choice—just make sure they get adequate sunlight. You can leave offerings of fresh-baked bread on your altar, place crystals associated with health and abundance around the perimeter, or whatever else feels appropriate. As with cooking itself, there are plenty of ways to be creative here!

You can dedicate one of your kitchen shelves to this purpose, or even use one of your cupboards if need be. However, if an altar isn't possible, or just isn't a fit with your particular spiritual path, there are other ways of creating sacred space in the kitchen—hang charms for protection or good luck from the ceiling or on the walls, burn incense or magical essential oils, or simply keep a charged candle burning in a safe place while you cook.

And whether you keep a permanent altar or not, always give consideration to the aesthetic quality of your kitchen overall. Keep things tidy as much as you can, so your focus isn't drawn to chaos and clutter when you walk into the room. Arrange dried herbs in attractive jars, and keep non-refrigerated produce in hanging baskets or arrange them in some other pleasing way.

See your kitchen as a living, ever-changing symbol of the bountiful harvest, noting and appreciating the evidence of abundance in your life on a daily basis. Doing so will help you maintain positive, harmonious vibrations throughout your kitchen.

Plants, as inherently magical beings in their own right, are always appropriate for kitchen decor, and many can be used directly in your practice of culinary magic. Basil, for example, is a delightfully pungent herb that also lends your kitchen protection from negative energy. Rosemary is a hardy herb with a wide variety of magical and culinary uses. Really, any herbs that do well in pots, such as parsley, chives, mint, and thyme, are excellent additions to your kitchen "garden," as all culinary herbs have magical uses.

Of course, not all of your kitchen plants need be culinary. For example, aloe vera, used for love, success and lunar magic, can protect against cooking mishaps as well as treat any minor kitchen burns or scrapes. Cacti, with their sunny, protective energies are wonderful additions, provided they get plenty of sunlight. For kitchens with low sunlight levels, spider plants are a great alternative. And if you want to attract the magic of the faeries, be sure to hang a fern or two from the ceiling.

Crystals are another great way to enhance the energy of your sacred hearth space. Place them on shelves, in cupboards, near the sink, or anywhere else where you'll see them regularly. Choose any that call to you, or look up stones with the magical properties of whatever you want to bring into your experience.

For example, amethyst's stress-relieving properties are helpful for transitioning from a long work day into a relaxed, magic-making frame of mind. Red jasper helps with the self-confidence and physical energy required to pull off a delicious magical meal. Citrine brings a sunny, abundant energy to your culinary work, while moonstone and blue topaz help to achieve and maintain a healthy diet. To enhance the well-being of your kitchen plants, bring in jade, moss agate, malachite, or any other green stones. And to enhance the taste of whatever you're preparing, keep a large quartz crystal near your oven.

For those who wish to work with ancient deities as part of their kitchen practice, whether as aspects of the God and Goddess or as separate deities in their own right, there are several possibilities to explore. As mentioned in Part One, the religious lives of our ancestors were inextricably bound with food and food production, so there are many, many deities associated with hearth and with agriculture.

Some of the most well-known hearth deities include the Greek goddess Hestia (and her Roman counterpart, Vesta) and the Celtic fire goddess Brighid, whose triple domains include smithcraft—forging tools in the fire—and who is often associated with the cauldron. The Roman god Vulcan can also be considered a hearth deity, as he is associated with fire and creativity—both essentials for successful kitchen magic.

One of the oldest agricultural deities is the Greek Mother goddess Gaia, who embodies the Earth, and provides all sustenance. The Celtic god Bres, husband of Brighid, also governs fertility and agriculture. The Egyptian god Osiris provides food for his people through the growing cycles of the banks of the Nile. Ra, who is the father of Osiris in some Egyptian myths, is associated with growth as a god of the light and warmth of the Sun. The many grain deities of the ancient world include the Greek goddess Demeter and her Roman equivalent, Ceres, in addition to the aforementioned Celtic god Lugh.

Plenty of other pantheons, such as those of Asian, African, and Native American cultures, have such deities as well, and their primary associations can easily be found with a little research. If you're interested in working with any ancient deity, be sure to read as much as you can about them before attempting to form a sacred connection.

ENCHANTING THE TINY KITCHEN: STUDIO APARTMENTS AND OTHER TRICKY KITCHEN SPACES

Arranging your kitchen for both optimal magic and ease of cooking can be a challenge even in the most spacious of kitchens, depending on the location of appliances, cabinets, etc. So what can you do if your "kitchen" is really just one corner of your studio apartment, or if it's a narrow space just big enough for a stove, sink and refrigerator? It certainly can be difficult to feel truly free and in the flow of magical energy in such tight spaces. But you can still get creative with your tiny kitchen.

If the kitchen is actually part of your living room, find a way to visually (and therefore energetically) designate the space. Perhaps you can paint the walls of this area a different color from the rest of the room, or place magical symbols and/or artwork on the cabinet doors. If you have to stand in tight spaces in order to cook, consider using small mirrors, à la feng shui, to energetically open up the space around you—you'll be surprised at the difference it makes! Corner shelves are excellent space-savers in small kitchens, and potentially good places for an altar.

If you want an altar but have absolutely no space for a permanent one, find a small area of the kitchen that can serve as a temporary altar for when you're actively working kitchen magic—or create an "extension" of the kitchen by pulling a small table up to the entrance and placing your magical items there.

Many people with tiny kitchens find that cooking complex, from-scratch meals is highly challenging, if not downright impossible, due to limited space. If this is your situation, don't despair. As discussed in Part One, what matters most is your focused intention as you work, whether you're making a gourmet feast or a simple, humble meal. Like many aspects of the Craft, kitchen witchery is a very personalized and adaptable practice. Do what you can with what you have, and above all, enjoy yourself!

CONSECRATING YOUR KITCHEN

Depending on your personal approach to magic and your own spiritual path, you may wish to perform a consecration ritual on your kitchen, dedicating it to the purpose of co-creating with the Universe in the form of culinary magic.

Of course, you will still use the kitchen for mundane activities—you don't necessarily have to have a magical mindset first thing in the morning when you're late for work and hastily grabbing a piece of toast. But this doesn't mean that you can't establish an ongoing feeling of sacred space within this very important room.

If you're Wiccan, you likely already have a method for consecrating ritual tools, which you can modify for use on a whole room rather than on a single object. Your ritual will likely involve honoring the God and Goddess in your own way. The Elements may be invited to take an active role in the work, each bringing its characteristic energies to create a balanced magical atmosphere in your hearth space. Depending on your practice, you may even make the consecration itself part of a larger ritual within your tradition.

If you follow another spiritual tradition that incorporates the blessing of a home or a specific space, you could apply those practices to your kitchen. Or you can simply invent your own approach. You may write out an elaborate ritual, addressing each major aspect of your kitchen (such as the oven, the pantry, etc.) or you might keep it simple, with a few words of gratitude and intention.

As a very personal undertaking, your approach to consecrating your kitchen has to be something that resonates with you. To give you a possible starting-off point, an example consecration ritual can be found in Part Three of this guide.

THE SHARED KITCHEN: "MUGGLES," CHILDREN, AND MESSY ROOMMATES

For single Witches who live alone, there is unlimited freedom to transform the kitchen into an ultra-magical space. For everyone else, however, it's often not that simple.

Those blessed enough to live with a magical partner or like-minded roommates may be able to engage the others in the household to contribute to the effort, creating a truly magical shared creative space in the kitchen. But for the Witch who lives with non-magically inclined people, maintaining an enchanted kitchen takes a special kind of creativity.

Despite the progress the Wiccan and other Pagan communities have made in the last few decades in terms of being accepted (or at least tolerated) in mainstream society, many people on the path of the Old Religion still feel the need to keep their practices a secret, even (or especially) from other family members. This is often the case for those whose family, friends, or roommates belong to one of the Abrahamic religions (Judaism, Christianity and Islam), and therefore have a misinformed view of the Craft.

If you're still "in the broom closet" when it comes to your spiritual practice, then how can you create and maintain sacred space in your shared kitchen?

First, know that you're in the company of generations who went before you, who lived and practiced in secret, and in extremely dangerous times at that. During the centuries when many Witches were executed for their way of life, anyone keeping to the old ways had to keep their practice an absolute secret, and likely would have hidden or disguised any tools of Witchcraft within their household.

This didn't prevent them from being able to work magic at the hearth, so there's no reason you can't do the same. The truth is, you don't absolutely need a physical altar or special symbols to imbue your shared kitchen with your own personal magical power. There are a number of ways to do so on the sly, without anyone in your household being any the wiser.

For example, you can certainly still clean your kitchen, holding the intention of clearing out unwanted energy while you work. If you have the house to yourself for a sufficient length of time, you can also bless the space with magical energy. Just be sure that your intention is not to manipulate the experience of others. Focus on enchanting the kitchen for yourself—the positive energy you create will likely have a beneficial effect on your housemates, provided you're not trying to *make* that happen.

You can also charge any object in the privacy of your room and place it in the kitchen as a talisman. Depending on who you live with, this could be a candle, a crystal, or a pretty stone you find while on a hike.

If even these items would raise eyebrows, try a house plant, a knick-knack, or a favorite mug—literally any ordinary object will do. It's great to be able to go all-out and make your kitchen a total Witch's haven, but know that you can also achieve magical results with incredible subtlety. As with any other kind of magic, it's not about the material things themselves, but rather your own personal intention and will.

Those who live with young children will already be accustomed to keeping potentially dangerous things out of their reach, so this precaution can obviously be extended to any ritual items or other magical objects you don't want disturbed by curious little hands. You may want to devote a high shelf to serve as an altar, or install one if there isn't room on the shelves you have. And since you probably don't get a lot of time to yourself in the kitchen (as opposed to people without children), you can try incorporating them into your work.

Children have incredible imaginations and a ton of creative energy—why not harness that power by asking them to participate? Ask them to put their love and magical energy into the steps they help with, whether that's stirring, rolling dough, or even just "playing cook" with their own toys alongside you while you work.

What about that roommate who has a knack for creating a total mess in the kitchen right after you've just cleaned it? Depending on the social dynamic in your household, you may want to start by communicating your desire to keep a tighter ship in this regard. If you're "out" as a Witch, this will probably be easier than if you keep your practice a secret, since you can explain that the quality of energy in the kitchen will affect the quality of everyone's meals, and not just yours.

Of course, dysfunctional living situations, where roommates don't have good communication, are unlikely to change just because you want to improve the energy of the kitchen. Nonetheless, it's worth giving it a try. In terms of magical solutions, you can do spellwork for a cleaner, more energetically conducive-to-magic kitchen, provided you're not trying to manipulate the behavior of others in your household. Spend time every day visualizing the kitchen as a clean, positive and welcoming space, without falling into resentment at the way it is now, and you'll be surprised at the changes that unfold.

Now that you've got your kitchen spic and span and blessed with magical energy, it's time to get out your culinary implements and start thinking and acting with a witchy perspective as you create transformative meals. Below, you'll find plenty of tips and suggestions for turning ordinary daily tasks into extraordinary magic.

MAGICAL THINKING: TOOLS AND TECHNIQUES OF KITCHEN WITCHERY

When it comes to thinking about magic, those who practice it as part of their spiritual path may automatically visualize an altar, ritual tools such as athames and pentacles, and/or the ingredients of spells such as oils, crystals, ribbons and sachets, etc. A successful practice of kitchen witchery, however, requires an ability to see the everyday objects found within the cupboards and drawers as also being magical.

Indeed, our ancestors made little distinction between "magical" and "mundane" when it came to acquiring and preparing food, and there's no reason for a modern kitchen witch to do so, either. Culinary magic is "practical magic" at its best, and once you learn to see every aspect of cooking with a magical eye, you'll be amazed at what a transformative process cooking can really be.

RE-ENVISIONING KITCHEN TOOLS

A great place to start is with the very practical, mundane objects and devices we use in order to prepare food. For those who work with ritual tools in Wicca or another Pagan practice, a few correlations will be fairly obvious—the chalice, the athame, the cauldron, etc. However, anything you work with in the process of making meals can be viewed symbolically for an enriched, esoteric cooking experience.

For example, consider the simple skillet. Given both its shape and function, we can consider this tool to have feminine, receptive qualities, though there's also an emphasis on transformation through the masculine Element of Fire. The skillet evokes the process of necessary change—its contents are refined by the heat until they are suitable for eating. This way of conceptualizing the use of a skillet is good for culinary magic related to personal transformation and meeting challenges successfully.

Spoons can be thought of as a kind of wand, balancing the energies of a given dish through the act of stirring the ingredients together. Depending on your magical goal, you might choose to stir in a clockwise (or "sunwise" direction) for increasing or attracting something into your life, or stir counterclockwise for releasing or banishing.

Another fairly obvious equivalence is between the cookbook and the grimoire, or Book of Shadows. Both contain treasure troves of knowledge that can be referred to again and again for inspiration and technical assistance. A fork can be seen as piercing exterior illusions and getting to the inner aspects of a problem or matter. A colander filters out what isn't needed in a situation so that only the useful and desired aspects remain.

These are all examples of how you can keep your focus on your intention as you work with your culinary tools to create edible magic. It's a metaphorical and essentially intuitive approach, and works entirely on an individual level. Try re-visioning your cooking methods through this magical lens, and once you find yourself making associative leaps, just run with it!

WORKING WITH CORRESPONDENCES

As has already been noted several times in this guide, your focused intention is the most important factor in the success of your magic. You will be infusing the individual ingredients of the meal with your own magical energy, no matter what the ingredients are or how you're using them in the work.

However, just as with spellwork, you can enhance the results of your culinary magic by choosing foods according to their magical associations, or correspondences. Just as you might work with patchouli oil, with its magical energies of prosperity, in a money spell, you can use barley, basil and/or pine nuts in a casserole dish to bring about the same results.

So how do you discover the magical correspondences of any given food? Research is always a good idea, but your own intuition should always be the final judge.

Magical correspondences come to us from ancient mythology and legends, as well as family traditions, medicinal knowledge, and personal experience. To take a random example, avocados are magically associated with love, lust and beauty and are used in spellwork to bring about or enhance these qualities in a person or a relationship.

This correspondence is likely connected to the belief systems of ancient Aztec and Mayan cultures associating avocados with the powers of attraction. One Aztec legend tells of how young, beautiful unmarried girls were kept indoors during the height of avocado season to protect them from men who were under the aphrodisiac spell of these rich, delicious fruits.

In early Western medicine, a concept known as the Doctrine of Signatures held that every plant that was useful to the body had a physical resemblance—or correspondence—to the part of the body it could heal. For example, the walnut has an uncanny resemblance to the human brain, and is widely known today to be highly beneficial to brain function. The original Greek name for the walnut is *caryon*, which translates to "head," and magical associations for this nut include wisdom and the conscious mind.

When it comes to discovering correspondences, there are plenty of online resources to consult, as well as a few trusted print sources, which will be listed on the recommended reading page at the end of this guide. Having this ancient wisdom at your fingertips is of great help as you build your kitchen witchery practice. However, the correspondences listed for any given food can vary from source to source, and ultimately the foods you choose to work with should make sense to you personally.

Don't feel that you need to use a specific ingredient just because a source you've consulted connects it with your goal. If you trust the source, great—that may be enough in many cases. But if you don't have a connection to the correspondence *within yourself*, the visualization/focused intention level isn't as strong.

In other words, if you're seeking new sources of prosperity, and your gut is telling you to make a carrot and sage soup, then by all means do so, regardless of whether you can find confirmation of this correspondence elsewhere. As you deepen your practice of kitchen witchery, you will likely start to intuit the best foods to work with at any given time, rather than having to do research for every magical meal.

One way to start building your own personal understanding about correspondences is to hold a food item in your hands and listen to what your intuition tells you regarding its ideal magical uses. You can also peruse your pantry with your magical goal in mind, and see which items immediately catch your eye. Just as experienced Witches find that specific herbs and crystals will "speak" to them when they're looking for ingredients to create a particular spell, you will likely find that certain foods in your pantry call to you when they are most likely to be useful in your magic.

If you want to take a simple but effective approach to correspondences, consider working according to the colors of different foods. You might use red and orange items (such as bell peppers and carrots) for work related to courage, strength and vitality; green foods (like spinach or snap peas) for prosperity; and purple foods (like cabbage or eggplant) for peace or wisdom.

Finally, if you already have personal established correspondences between certain foods and aspects of life, then by all means work with them. You might, for example, associate cherries with wisdom or familial love if you had a wise grandmother who made cherry pie for you when you came to visit her. Or a favorite food discovered on a vacation might be permanently connected to feelings of joy, freedom or enlightenment.

The experiences of your life and the way they shape your perceptions of food, along with your own intuition, are ultimately more important than any stated correspondence in any magical resource, no matter how trustworthy.

CHOOSING MAGICAL MENUS

When you think about all the possibilities that kitchen witchery presents, finding a place to start might seem a little overwhelming. Even if you have a specific magical goal, the options for incorporating it into a meal are pretty vast— especially if you're an experienced cook.

To help you narrow down your choices, try taking a simple approach: start with what you know and what you like to eat. Often, rather than having to seek out new recipes that fit with your magical goals, you can simply examine the correspondences of ingredients in dishes you already eat, and tailor them to maximize their magical potency for manifesting your desire. You'll find an example of how to do this below.

One way to incorporate magic into your diet on a regular basis is to work with the season you're in. What's locally available right now? If you don't have access to locally-grown food, think in terms of the next upcoming Sabbat before your next trip to the grocery store. Look to the traditional foods associated with that Sabbat and find (or invent) recipes featuring those foods. Then examine the correspondences or symbolic significance of the ingredients to see which of your current magical goals they align with, and take it from there.

Whether or not you're a practicing Wiccan, eating with the Wheel of the Year helps you attune on an energetic level with the turning of the seasons, whether or not you're incorporating spellwork into the meals. You'll find a few resources for eating according to the seasons on the recommended reading page at the end of this guide.

Along these lines, you can also work with the phases of the Moon, making food aligned with increase (prosperity, fertility, etc.) during the waxing phase and meals for banishing or decrease (healing from illness, resolving arguments) during the waning phase. Consider a monthly feast celebrating the current sign of the Zodiac with foods related to the strengths of that particular sign. If you're well-versed in astrology, you can extend this approach to any significant planetary transits, trines, or other configurations, such as a meal focused on honoring Mercury in retrograde.

No matter how you go about planning a magical menu, always keep in mind that vibrational frequency is key to attracting the circumstances you desire. If you're forcing yourself to eat something you don't like, then you won't be at the right frequency for the spell to do its work.

On a related note, however, using magical correspondences and seasonal influences can be a great way to discover new foods that you've never tried before. Perhaps you want to make a magical meal to help you land a new job, but can't find many correspondences among the foods you typically eat. This is an ideal circumstance for experimenting with something new.

When you find new foods that you like, there's an extra boost of joyful energy from your new discovery that can make for incredibly powerful magic!

TIPS, TWEAKS, AND WITCHY KITCHEN HACKS

Whether you're a beginning cook, a seasoned recipe-follower, or a maestro improvisational chef, there's always room to learn new methods and enhance your kitchen witchery practice. Here are a few suggestions for creative ways to take your culinary magic up a notch:

Substitutions and Additions

Depending on the type of food you're working with and your level of cooking experience, there are often opportunities to switch out or add ingredients to boost a standard recipe's magical power.

For example, you might use thyme instead of rosemary in a stew for more psychic energy, or top a tray of roasted vegetables with chopped cashews to increase your income. Just be careful not to alter the taste of the food to the extent that you won't want to eat it, since you do need to enjoy the meal for it to have magical impact.

Water Work

Intentionally charged drinking water is a fairly well-known technique among Witches and other magical practitioners. Cooking involves the use of water so often that it seems a waste not to take advantage of this Elemental influence.

Get in the habit of blessing any water that will end up infusing the food somehow, whether it's for soaking beans, cooking pasta, rice, or other grains, steaming vegetables, etc. You can also charge herbs for your magical purpose and toss them into cooking water.

Using a few drops of a crystal elixir is another creative possibility. Just make sure you work with stones that are safe for the body. There are many crystals used in other forms of magic that are toxic when ingested, so do your research first!

Symbolism

Symbols are a central component in all kinds of magic—in fact, all magic could be said to work through the power of symbolism in one way or another. Try incorporating symbols into your edible creations where possible—carve dollar signs, hearts, runes, etc. into baked goods and "draw" symbols onto sandwiches and pancakes with condiments (ketchup, maple syrup, etc.)

You can also arrange appetizers and sides, such as chips and fruit slices, into symbols on the plate. Taking this even further, you can use the symbolic power of numbers to enhance the experience of preparing and eating the meal. For example, sprinkle oregano into a sauce 3 times to honor the Triple Goddess, place 9 cherry tomatoes on a salad for promoting growth, or ladle 4 generous spoonfuls of soup into each bowl to honor the Elements or celebrate creativity.

Keeping it Simple: Magical Flavor Boosts

Not every meal has to be an elaborate, premeditated magical production (although the results of such sessions tend to be well worth the effort!). You can integrate kitchen witchery into your normal cooking routine as well.

Pre-charged creations like herbal tinctures, spice blend packets, pesto cubes, infused oils, homemade salad dressings, etc. can be made ahead of time and kept on hand for spur-of-the-moment culinary magic. Add to pastas, salads, soups or whatever else you're cooking for an extra dash of magical energy on the fly.

Furthermore, if you're making a meal that includes more than one dish, know that it doesn't *all* have to be dedicated to your magical goals. You can focus your intention into the salad or side dish that accompanies the main course, or even dessert. Kitchen magic shouldn't feel like an overwhelming endeavor— in fact, if it does become stressful, you're unlikely to get the results you seek. So take it easy, have fun, and do what you can as your schedule (and ability level) allows.

PUTTING IT TOGETHER

Now that you've got some ideas for how to transform your kitchen into a magical space, choose foods in accordance with your magical goals, and view the cooking process through a magical lens, it's time to look at a specific example of kitchen witchery.

Next, we'll take a fairly simple staple of Western cuisine— marinara sauce—and examine step-by-step how you can apply what you've learned so far about the magical energy of food and how to approach cooking from your new witchy perspective.

This is not a specific recipe, but rather a set of broad guidelines for how you can select ingredients according to your magical goal, charge them with your personal energy, and put them to use in manifesting the change you're seeking, all while creating a delicious sauce for an enchanting meal.

MAGICAL MARINARA SAUCE

Marinara sauce is perhaps one of the most popular foods in modern Western civilization. It's also often referred to as "spaghetti sauce," as spaghetti is the pasta most frequently eaten with marinara, but you can actually use this sauce on any type of pasta, as well as on polenta and even on pizza. (In the case of pizza, however, the sauce is generally not cooked ahead of time.)

There is no shortage of recipes for marinara out there and there is plenty of variation among them, but in general, a sauce fitting the "marinara" category will be comprised chiefly of tomatoes, with a handful of other ingredients for seasoning. (A "chunky" marinara may also contain additional vegetables for a more robust sauce.)

The relative simplicity of most marinara recipes, along with the opportunities to customize the sauce to your own liking—and your own magical goals—makes this a good dish to use as an illustration of magical cooking. So even if you're not a fan of anything remotely resembling Italian food, read on for a more in-depth sense of how you can use the principles outlined in this guide in your own personalized kitchen witchery practice.

INGREDIENTS

As you consider ingredients for your magical marinara, remember that "fresh is best" in terms of prana, or universal life-force.

Depending on the season and your location, you may have access to incredibly fresh, locally-grown, "high-vibrational" tomatoes as well as just-picked herbs and vegetables to create a delicious sauce from. (For example, there's a variety of tomatoes known as "Mountain Magic" that has become increasingly popular at local farmers' markets!) On the other hand, you may need to rely on non-local produce or even canned tomatoes—this is perfectly fine.

In fact, if it's winter where you live, you might want to pass on any "fresh" tomatoes at your grocery store—especially if they're conventionally grown. These tomatoes have been picked too early in the ripening process, are often tasteless, and tend to feel very low-vibrational in terms of prana. So if these are the only tomatoes in your store, you're probably better off using quality organic canned tomatoes instead.

And if you're just not ready to try a from-scratch recipe for your marinara, there's no harm in using pre-made sauce from a jar! Just be sure to add your own magical touch to store-bought marinara by including fresh or dried herbs and/or other seasonings, focusing your personal energy into every particle of the sauce as you do so. (We'll discuss this further, below.)

Next, decide on seasonings for your magical concoction. You'll almost certainly want some combination of basil, oregano, parsley, thyme, and/or garlic. Fresh herbs are wonderful when you can get them, but dried herbs are just as effective when it comes to magic, as any herbally-inclined Witch will tell you.

If you're making your sauce from scratch, you may also want to include bay leaves, red pepper flakes, lemon juice, cornstarch for thickening, and/or sugar or honey to reduce the tartness of the tomatoes, as well as a chopped, sautéed onion. Additional vegetables could include zucchini or summer squash, mushrooms, carrots, bell peppers, etc. (Note: you can also add veggies to a pre-made sauce by sautéing them in olive oil first and stirring in the sauce once they've softened.)

If this is your first time making a from-scratch marinara, it's strongly recommended that you find a recipe to follow, so your energy and attention can be focused on your magical techniques, with a fair amount of confidence that the sauce will turn out well!

CORRESPONDENCES AND MAGICAL GOALS

What is magical marinara sauce used for, in terms of kitchen witchery? There's no one single answer to this question, since there are many different magical properties associated with every ingredient you could possibly put in it.

For example, the tomatoes alone can be used in magic relating to love, protection, health or money. If you choose thyme for a seasoning, you might draw on its associations with psychic awareness, purification, or attracting loyalty. Basil, on the other hand, can be used for prosperity or protection.

This diversity within the magical energies of food is at the heart of the creative potential of culinary magic. It's also part of what makes it so practical! With this variety of possibilities in mind, let's take a look at some of the known magical correspondences for each of the ingredients you might include in a marinara sauce:

Vegetables

Tomatoes: money, health, attracting love, protection
Onion: protection, prosperity, clearing away obstacles
Zucchini/squash: spirituality, fertility
Mushrooms: psychic awareness
Carrots: vision, sex, masculine energies
Bell peppers: Green—prosperity; Red—vitality, strength; Yellow—creativity

Herbs

Garlic: health, protection, banishing, breaking hexes
Basil: money, loving vibrations, protection, wards off negativities in a home
Oregano: peace, deepening love relationships, releasing old relationships
Parsley: protection (specifically from accidents), money, luck, lust, strength, vitality
Thyme: love, affection, attracting loyalty, courage, psychic awareness, purification
Red pepper flakes: deflecting negative energy, avoiding unpleasant people
Bay leaf: good fortune, money, success, protection, purification, strength, psychic awareness

Other Ingredients

Olive oil: peace, health, protection, spirituality, sex, fertility, fidelity
Sugar: love, affection, banishing gossip

Honey: health, happiness, love, lust, sex, purification, wisdom, stability

Lemon juice: love, longevity, purification, marriage, happiness, faithfulness

Cornstarch: protection, harmony with Earth, luck, abundance

As you can see, there are many different goals you could focus on as you create your magical marinara. However, some goals have a greater likelihood of success than others, depending on the magical properties of all the ingredients you choose to include.

For example, yellow bell peppers are associated with creativity, and adding some chopped yellow pepper charged with this intention could certainly have an impact. But if your desire is truly to increase your creativity, then it might make more sense to create a dish that features yellow peppers and/or other foods associated with creativity more prominently than a marinara sauce typically would.

Indeed, focusing on something that's represented in as many ingredients as possible is ideal for maximizing the meal's magical energy. And since the main ingredient in marinara sauce is tomatoes, it makes the most sense to work for a goal associated with one of the magical attributes of tomatoes. With this in mind, let's look at how you might concoct a magical marinara for the purposes of manifesting money, health, love, or protection.

If your intent is to attract money, you'll definitely want to include basil and parsley in your sauce, as well as a bay leaf or two. Onions and green bell peppers are also good additions here, as is zucchini squash, with its green color and association with fertility which can be applied to one's business or investments.

For health-related goals, be sure to use plenty of garlic and olive oil, and consider sweetening the sauce with a bit of honey. In addition, a quick squeeze of lemon juice, for longevity, helps bring out the flavor of the tomatoes.

Of course, it's worth noting here that *any* food that is high in prana and prepared with positive intention is suitable for health-related goals, since what we eat is a primary factor in our overall health. However, it can still be fun to zero in on foods traditionally associated with good health when it comes to magical dishes.

When it comes to love-related goals, you can choose ingredients according to the particular situation you're wanting to attract. Thyme and basil are excellent for bringing the energies of love and affection into your life, while parsley, carrots and olive oil are more associated with lust and sex. Olive oil is also known for encouraging fidelity, and oregano is used for releasing old relationships and strengthening existing ones.

The sweetness of sugar makes it probably the most obvious of love-associated ingredients, and it can be used here to temper the acidity of the tomatoes. (Raw or brown sugar is recommended over refined white sugar.) Honey is an excellent alternative to sugar, as it also has associations with love, as does lemon juice, which is often found in recipes for marinara and even in many brands of canned tomatoes.

While bay leaves are not primarily associated with love, they *are* associated with success and good fortune. This makes them great all-purpose magical ingredients—simply charge them with your specific intention, and let their magical energy infuse the sauce!

Many of the ingredients discussed here so far are also associated with protection. In addition to the tomatoes, we find protective qualities in basil, parsley, bay leaf, garlic, olive oil, onion and even cornstarch. As with love-related goals, you can do some further research to tailor your choices to your specific circumstances.

If you're seeking protection from accidents, use parsley. If you're warding off illness, use garlic. Garlic is also good for protection from unwanted energies in the home, as is basil. There are other protective herbs and seasonings not mentioned above that can also go well in a marinara sauce, such as salt, black pepper, marjoram and rosemary. Each of these has their own particular "flavor" of protective energy, guarding against a range of unwanted experiences, from general negativity to jealousy to theft.

Another option in a customizable dish like marinara sauce is to work with the magical associations of a key secondary ingredient, with the intention that the energy of the ingredient (as well as other complimentary ingredients) becomes the magical focus of the meal.

For example, if you want to make a sauce that emphasizes mushrooms, you could decide to focus on the psychic energies of these delectable edible fungi. Include a bay leaf and some thyme, and you've got three ingredients associated with boosting psychic awareness.

As you can see, there are many options for choosing a magical goal for a dish with multiple ingredients. All it takes is a little research into magical correspondences along with your own creativity and intuition!

As for what you'll be serving your marinara with—whether it's pasta, polenta or something else—this is, of course, entirely up to you. Depending on your purposes, you may see this component as an integral part of the overall magical dish, or you may focus your intent into the sauce alone, which will then cover whatever is served underneath it. This is a perfectly fine approach—not every single part of a given meal needs to be magically prepared.

However, you might enjoy incorporating, for example, the traditional Chinese association between long noodles and long life, luck, and success into your dish. Others have associated spaghetti and linguini with protection, while spiral pasta is said to enhance creativity. If your goal is a new job or business opportunity, try using bowtie pasta. If you're more of a polenta person, you could draw on any of the magical properties associated with corn, such as protection, luck, abundance, or divination, just to name a few.

Finally, when it comes to choosing ingredients, this bit of advice is worth repeating: make sure you enjoy what you're preparing! This is crucial to the success of your magic. If you're working for prosperity but hate green peppers, then by all means leave them out of your marinara sauce, regardless of the correspondence. You can focus your intention on the money energies of the basil, parsley, bay leaf, etc. instead.

CHARGE, COOK, ENJOY

Once you've decided on a goal for your culinary magic and the specific ingredients for your dish, you're ready to put your kitchen witchery into practice.

First, always be sure to "set the stage" for magic, just as if you were preparing for ritual and/or other types of spellwork. Light a candle or two and put on some inspiring music. You might want to light some incense or place a few drops of essential oils on an oil burner. Spending a few moments quieting your mind and letting go of your day is essential, especially if you've been busy or under any stress.

Do whatever you need to do to create for yourself a sense of ease and wonder as you transform an otherwise mundane "household chore" into a magical experience—remember, your kitchen is now an enchanted space! And just as you would gather your ingredients prior to spellwork, be sure to get out everything you need for preparing the meal—including all kitchen implements and cookware—so you won't be interrupted in your magical focus by having to dash for something at the last minute.

Now it's time to charge your ingredients. There are many ways to do this, and you may already have your own preferred method(s) based on your personal experience with spellwork.

When it comes to kitchen magic, one very practical way is to simply hold the ingredients between your palms. This works particularly well with fresh vegetables and fruit, as their relatively high water content, in addition to their high degree of prana, makes them very receptive to absorbing your energy.

Take a deep breath, and as you exhale, visualize your personal energy infusing the food with your magical intention. You might also visualize a specific color in association with your goal flowing into the item, such as green for prosperity or orange for courage, or you might simply call upon the prana of the food to connect with you and your desire. You can do this silently, or you can speak some brief words aloud. For example:

"I call on the life force energy of (name ingredient) to assist me with manifesting (name magical goal)."

If you're using canned tomatoes, simply hold the can between your palms and send your energy into the food within. (Whenever possible, remove the lids of cans, jars and bottles for closer energetic proximity to the ingredients within.) If you're using a pre-made sauce, then hold the jar and visualize each of the ingredients being activated with your personal power.

You may wish to acknowledge each ingredient according to its role in your spellwork—for example, tomatoes for promoting good health and garlic for protection from illness. As with any other aspect of magic, this is all entirely up to you and what feels appropriate in your experience. In fact, the specific approach you use for charging ingredients is not important at all—all that matters is your ability to focus your personal magical energy into the food for its intended purpose.

If the prospect of charging each and every ingredient before the cooking even begins sounds daunting, know that in most cases, you can actually do this step in advance. Just as you might need to charge crystals or candles a day or two ahead of a Full Moon spell, time constraints might require you to charge ingredients for magical meals when you bring them home from the grocery store.

This is fine, though some people like to hold off on charging fresh produce until after they've rinsed it, to keep as much of their energetic imprint on the food as possible. Furthermore, you don't have to individually charge every single item— holding a handful of tomatoes or a few cloves of garlic and charging them all at once is perfectly effective.

Remember, ultimately this process should be enjoyable, rather than tedious. Keep your focus on maintaining a high vibrational frequency and approach each magical action in a way that delights you.

Once your ingredients are charged, proceed with making your marinara as you normally would, but with a continued focus on your magical goal. If you're slicing vegetables, for example, you might envision the energy of each slice infusing the overall sauce with its inherent magical vitality. If you're adding multiple herbs to the sauce all at once, place them in a bowl or mortar first and mix them together with your fingertips—this is a particularly powerful step in many herbal spells. If you're sautéing onions for the base of the sauce, visualize the magical energies of olives and onions fusing together and strengthening the potency of the dish.

If you like, speak spell words, incantations, invocations to the Elements, or anything else that fits your magical style. Do the same with any other vegetables you add, as well as with herbs, sugar, or other additions to the marinara—each item you bring into the mix is adding its own energies to create a nourishing, delicious manifestation of your desires.

You can make this process as simple or as elaborate as you like—the important thing is to stay focused on your goal from start to finish. Don't be running through the details of your day or worrying about the future—stay in the present moment. And be sure to taste the food as you go, noting the changes made by each addition to the sauce and appreciating the ongoing transformation of these raw ingredients into a magical meal.

If you're using a pre-made jar of marinara, then obviously you don't have as many opportunities to visualize your intended manifestation during the cooking process. But this doesn't mean you can't infuse your meal with magic all the same.

First, as mentioned above, charge the jar of sauce before beginning your work, visualizing each of the ingredients being infused with your magical energy. Then you'll need to pour the sauce into a saucepan and heat it up gently. (If you're adding vegetables, sauté them in olive oil first, visualizing intently as you do so.)

Even if the sauce already tastes great, be sure to add something to it that you've charged with your magical intention, whether it's fresh or dried herbs, sugar, honey, or lemon juice to punch up the flavor. Make it as much of an original creation as possible—you can even drizzle some magically charged olive oil over some fresh crusty bread to accompany your meal!

When your marinara is ready (along with the pasta or whatever it is you're serving it with), it's important to take a moment to truly appreciate your magical creation before digging in.

If you already have a tradition of praying over your food before you eat, then this step is already built in, but if not, be sure to incorporate a statement or two of gratitude into your kitchen witchery practice. You might wish to acknowledge the Goddess and God or the Elements, and say a few words about the magical goal you're seeking to manifest. Or you could keep it simple with something like the following:

"I give thanks to the bounty of Mother Earth for this life-giving and transformative meal. Blessed Be."

As you eat, be sure to appreciate the taste of the food, the magical work it's accomplishing, and yourself for putting in the time and effort to create the meal. Stay focused on this enjoyment, remembering the importance of vibrational frequency to magical work. Don't eat in front of the TV or scroll through messages on your phone—be present with your food.

When you're finished, it's a good idea to "seal" your culinary spellwork with an acknowledgment of the physical processes of digestion, here on the Earth plane, that contribute to the manifestation of your goal. For example, since digestion involves each of the Elements, you might say something like this:

> *"By the powers of Earth, Water, Air and Fire,*
> *I now manifest the goal that I desire."*

You could also tailor these words more specifically to the goal you're working for, if you like. The main thing is to mentally connect, one final time, the magical energy of the food you've prepared and eaten with the energy of your physical body.

From an esoteric perspective, this simple act of creating a nourishing dish with focused intention —whether it's marinara, beans and rice, or broccoli casserole— is a very practical way to employ the Hermetic principles discussed in Part One. By choosing as many fresh, high-in-prana ingredients as possible (and choosing high-quality canned/packaged foods when necessary) and keeping a cheerful, relaxed mood throughout the process, you are utilizing the Principle of Vibration to your best advantage.

Likewise, by focusing on your intention as you charge the ingredients, and visualizing your desired outcome with each step of the cooking process, you are connecting yourself and your goal with the Universal mind via the Principle of Mentalism. Finally, by eating and enjoying the meal you are taking in the inherent magical properties of specific foods (the microcosm) and incorporating them into your body (the macrocosm) to obtain specific results—is an excellent way to employ the Principle of Correspondence.

But whether these specific concepts ever cross your mind while you're in the kitchen doesn't actually matter. As long as you're focused, energized, and having fun, you're bound to experience success in your practice of culinary magic!

MOVING FORWARD WITH YOUR PRACTICE

Hopefully, the discussions above regarding enchanting your kitchen and re-visioning the cooking process, as well as the example of magical cooking, have given you a sense of the endless possibilities and potential for creativity when it comes to kitchen witchery. You are now more than ready to begin your own personalized practice of this ancient Craft, but there will always be more to learn!

In Part Three, you'll find even more inspiration for transforming the mundane into the magical, including a few sample recipes; spells for enhancing your practice; tables of correspondence for basic pantry staples, common food colors, and Elemental influences; and further miscellaneous ideas for making the most out of the magical energies of your food. So read on, and enjoy this mini kitchen grimoire!

SECTION THREE

A KITCHEN
GRIMOIRE

BLESSINGS, RECIPES AND FURTHER INFORMATION FOR THE MAGICAL COOK

Centuries before Wicca and other modern forms of the Craft came into being, magical texts were often known as "grimoires." These books, often handed down from one generation to the next in secret, contained spells, rituals, and other magical information often dating back to ancient times.

Cookbooks also have an ancient lineage, and many of them would have combined culinary and magical information, since food and magic were not seen as separate domains until just a couple of centuries ago.

The collection of information below is a mini version of what an ancient culinary grimoire might have contained, though very much updated for the modern world. Use it as a starting point for creating your own personal magical cookbook, adding and changing details as you experiment to find what works best for you.

ELEMENTAL KITCHEN CONSECRATION RITUAL

Here is an example consecration ritual that can be used by Wiccans and non-Wiccans alike.

The universal energies of the Elements are called upon to enhance the magical atmosphere you'll be creating in your kitchen. If you wish, you can also include language that incorporates the Goddess and the God or any other deities you have a spiritual connection with.

It's best to perform this ritual after a thorough deep clean of your kitchen, but if that's just not possible, don't let it stop you. Just clean as much as you can beforehand. Smudge with sage, rosemary, and/or lavender before beginning the blessing.

The herbs suggested for this ritual all double as kitchen spices and are associated with purification, protection, good luck and/or success. The list of options below it not remotely exhaustive, however, so if there are other herbs you'd prefer to work with, by all means do so!

Depending on the layout of your kitchen, you may not be able to place each Element candle directly on the floor in the center of each wall. If this is the case, just place the candle as close to this spot as possible, even if it has to be on a countertop, a shelf, or even on top of the fridge.

You will need:

- Earth candle (green or brown)
- Fire candle (red or orange)
- Air candle (yellow or white)
- Water candle (blue or silver)

- White spell candle
- Mortar or bowl
- Consecration incense or a few drops of essential oil (heated with an oil burner or diffuser) with one or more of the following ingredients:
  - Frankincense
  - Myrrh
  - Sandalwood
  - Jasmine
  - Rose
  - Ylang ylang
  - Cinnamon
  - Lavender
  - Lemon
- 4 bay leaves (good fortune, success)
- 1 whole star anise (consecration, purification, luck)
- 1 whole cinnamon stick (consecration, success)
- 1 teaspoon each of four of the following herbs:
  - Clove (protection, good luck)
  - Basil (purification, protection)
  - Cumin (protection)
  - Dill (protection)
  - Fennel seed (purification, protection)
  - Rosemary (purification, protection)
  - Thyme (purification)
- 4 small token representations of foods you really like: e.g., a pinto bean, a dried cranberry, a piece of dry pasta, a small piece of bread, etc.

Instructions:

Gather all of your ingredients and place the incense or essential oil and the white spell candle on a surface that serves as a focal point—your kitchen altar, if you have one, or a table or countertop.

Take a deep breath, exhale, and light the incense or oil.

Place each Element candle on the floor at the center of the wall that most closely aligns with its directional association, in the following order: Earth in the north, Air in the east, Fire in the south, and Water in the west.

Now, light the Earth candle and place a bay leaf in front of it. Do the same with the Air, Fire, and Water candles.

As you do so, verbally acknowledge the power of the Element as it relates to food and food preparation in the home, using the following (or similar) words:

Earth: *"I welcome the energies of abundant sustenance into my kitchen."*
Air: *"I welcome the energies of the invisible life force into my kitchen."*
Fire: *"I welcome the energies of nourishing transformation into my kitchen."*
Water: *"I welcome the energies of life-sustaining flow into my kitchen."*

Next, place the four teaspoons of your chosen herbs in the mortar or bowl.

Mix the herbs together with your fingers and then stir them with the cinnamon stick three times in a clockwise (sunwise) direction.

Briefly dip each food token into the herb mixture and place it on one of the bay leaves.

Briefly dip the star anise into the herb mixture, then place it in front of the white spell candle.

As you prepare to light the candle, take a deep breath, exhale, and say the following (or similar) words:

"Working in union with the powers of Earth, Air, Fire and Water,
and with the sacred Fifth Element of Spirit,
I bless this kitchen.

This room is now my sacred hearth space
where magic is made with joyful intention,
nourishing the body, mind and soul.
Blessed Be."

Now light the candle and spend a few moments in quiet reflection.

When you feel that the consecration work is done, take the food tokens, bay leaves and herb mixture outdoors and sprinkle them over the Earth.

The star anise and cinnamon stick can be used later in magical recipes or kept as lucky kitchen charms. The Element candles can be gently extinguished and used again in other ritual work or just for ambience. Leave the white spell candle to burn out safely on its own.

BLESSING BEFORE A MEAL

Perhaps one of the most universal spiritual practices going back to the earliest humans is the act of praying over food before eating it.

Giving thanks to the creator from whom ultimately all things come—whether that's the God and Goddess, the Earth, the Universe, or however you envision Source—is not only spiritually "polite," but it's also a form of acknowledging the abundance in your life, which helps reinforce and attract more abundance. The act of blessing a meal has also traditionally been a way to ensure that the food itself will nourish the body and prevent illness.

Many cultures and religious traditions pray over every meal of the day, whereas others save this practice for the evening meal. Your approach to this custom is entirely up to you, and it's certainly not mandatory for a practice of kitchen witchery.

However, if you would like to incorporate this into your practice and aren't sure how to go about it, here is an example meal blessing that you can borrow and/or alter however you wish:

"Gratitude to the God and Goddess
who make manifest all of this goodness.
May the food before me nourish me
in body, mind and soul, and may each day
bring forth such abundance.
Blessed Be."

EDIBLE MAGIC: A SAMPLING OF RECIPES

These simple recipes can be tailored to your magical goals if you want to switch out an ingredient or two. However, if you're a beginning cook (or beginning magician), you might want to try them out as-is first.

FORTIFICATION VEGGIE SOUP

Almost every main ingredient in this soup is magically associated with protection. Secondary associations of several ingredients include health, strength, and peace. You are also shoring up your physical health with the nutritional value of each ingredient, bringing protection from illness.

Vegetable stock (or vegetable bouillon dissolved in water) is recommended, but if you can't find any, water will work fine. You may want to increase the rosemary and other seasonings if using water.

Note: The key to making delicious soups is in tasting your concoction as you add your seasonings. Doing so can also help you keep your focus on your magical goal!

Ingredients:

- 2 tablespoons olive oil
- 1 cup chopped onions
- 2 cups chopped leeks
- 3 garlic cloves, minced
- 2 tablespoons chopped fresh rosemary
- 2 cups peeled and sliced carrots
- 2 cups fingerling potatoes, chopped
- 6 cups water or vegetable stock
- 1 bay leaf
- 1 to 3 teaspoons dried thyme, sage, oregano and/or marjoram
- 3 cups rinsed and chopped kale
- 1 to 2 cups cooked lentils
- ½ to 1 teaspoon lemon juice, red wine vinegar or apple cider vinegar

- Salt and ground black pepper to taste

Instructions:

In a large soup pot, heat the oil and add the onions, leeks and garlic.

Cover and sauté on medium heat for 5 to 7 minutes, stirring frequently.

When the onions are soft, add the rosemary, carrots and potatoes and stir for 1 minute.

Add the water or stock and bay leaf.

Cover and bring to a boil, then reduce heat to simmer for 10 minutes.

Add the dried herbs and kale and simmer for 5 to 10 more minutes, until all the vegetables are tender.

Add the lentils and lemon juice or vinegar, then season with salt and pepper to taste.

Makes 4 servings.

LUCKY MONEY STIR-FRY

Many of the ingredients below are associated with money, including the peanuts and ginger as well as all of the green veggies! Be sure to have all of your prep work done in advance, as you'll need to be stirring constantly once you've heated the oil.

Ingredients:

- 1 tablespoon coconut oil
- 1 chopped onion
- 1 to 2 minced chili peppers
- 1 cup chopped broccoli
- 1 cup chopped cabbage
- 1 cup chopped carrots
- 1 cup chopped shiitake mushrooms
- 1 cup chopped green bell peppers
- 1 cup chopped snow peas
- 8 ounces shelled peanuts
- 1 tablespoon minced garlic
- 1 tablespoon minced ginger
- 1-2 tablespoons thinly sliced scallions

Sauce:

- 2 tablespoons soy sauce
- 1 tablespoon rice vinegar
- 1 tablespoon honey
- (whisk together in a bowl until smooth)

Instructions:

Heat the oil in a wok or skillet over high heat.

Test heat by dropping one piece of onion into the oil—when it sizzles, the oil is ready.

Add the rest of the onion and stir-fry for 1 minute.

Add the chili peppers, broccoli, cabbage, and carrots and stir-fry for 3 to 4 minutes.

Add the mushrooms, bell peppers, snow peas and peanuts and stir-fry for 3 to 4 minutes, until vegetables are tender-crisp.

Add the garlic and ginger and stir-fry for 30 to 45 seconds.

Add the sauce and stir-fry for one minute.

Remove the pan from the heat and serve over rice.

Makes 2 to 3 servings.

TROPICAL LOVE SMOOTHIE

Most fruits have love as one of their magical associations, so if you're not crazy about mango and/or pineapple, feel free to make substitutions. This sweet recipe makes roughly one serving, so just double it if sharing with someone special.

Ingredients:

- 1 medium fresh banana, peeled and sliced
- 2/3rds cup coconut/almond milk blend
- ½ cup frozen, roughly chopped mango
- ½ cup frozen, roughly chopped pineapple
- 1 teaspoon maple syrup
- ¼ teaspoon vanilla extract

Instructions:

Place all ingredients in a blender or food processor.

Pulse a few times to mix ingredients, then blend on high until smooth (usually 1 to 2 minutes).

SUCCESSFUL SESAME SALAD DRESSING

The bright, beaming energies of lemon and sesame come together in this easy dressing. Sesame's many magical associations include success and abundance, attracting new opportunities, and renewing hope. Lemon juice brings an uplifting, happy vibration to any recipe, but is particularly powerful here due to its prominence.

Note: you may need up to 6 lemons to get 6 tablespoons of juice, depending on how ripe the lemons are, but the work of squeezing the juice yourself is absolutely worth it!

Ingredients:

- 2/3rds cup tahini (sesame seed paste)
- 2 medium garlic cloves, minced or pressed
- 6 tablespoons fresh squeezed lemon juice
- ½ teaspoon salt
- 5-7 tablespoons water

Instructions:

Mix the tahini, garlic, lemon juice and salt together with a whisk or fork until smoothly blended.

Then slowly stir in the water, only adding enough to thin the mixture to a pourable consistency.

Let the dressing sit for 20 minutes before using.

It will keep in a clean, tightly closed jar for up to 4 days.

VERSATILE MAGICAL FOODS

When you work with natural, whole foods like fruits and vegetables, you're often interacting with them in multiple ways (washing, peeling, chopping, separating the edible parts from the inedible parts, etc.) before you add them to the dish you're preparing. Many of these foods offer opportunities to work a little magic in the process of preparing them for cooking. Here are just a few examples:

Bay Leaves

Many recipes for soups and sauces call for bay leaves, which are associated with protection, purification, healing, strength, good fortune, money, and success.

Witches commonly use bay leaves in wish magic, writing their wish on a bay leaf and burning, burying, or placing it under their pillow. When it comes to cooking, charging a bay leaf with the energy of your focused intention before adding it to the pot brings a little magic to the dish, even if the overall meal is just a "normal" weeknight dinner. The leaf infuses the liquid with its flavor as well as its inherent magical energy.

To take this technique a step further, you can charge the bay leaf and then rub a thin layer of olive oil across it with your forefinger. Then, with a chopstick or other clean, pointed tool, write a word or draw a symbol that represents your wish. Visualize your desired outcome as you drop the leaf into the pot. (Don't forget to remove it before you eat—whether or not you're using it magically.)

Onions

Onions have potent medicinal and magical attributes. They are found in an enormous variety of savory dishes around the world, and in several different types of spellwork. Onions may be cut and buried for love spells or banishings, and some people add onion skins to incense for banishing as well as attracting money.

The act of peeling an onion in a magical mindset can enhance any magical meal you're preparing. It's particularly good for magic related to healing, clearing obstacles, dispelling negative emotions, and doing away with any unwanted influences. The next time you're cooking with onion, try visualizing the peeling process as a means of releasing what's no longer needed in order to get to the core of what you're seeking.

Lemons

With their cheerful yellow rinds, lemons emanate undeniably positive and vibrant energy. Added to soups, stews, beverages and much more, lemon juice plays many different culinary roles.

In magic, lemons are used for healing, longevity, purification and spiritual awareness, among other goals. Using fresh-squeezed lemon juice in your recipes is well worth the effort, and allows you to take advantage of the seeds and the peel for spellwork.

The act of squeezing the lemons can also become a small ritual in and of itself. Imagine that the juice pouring forth from the fruit is akin to the unseen blessings of the Universe now coming into your life, as a result of the co-creation between Nature's processes and your own effort. Allow yourself to feel gratitude for what is already good in your life, and the excitement of knowing there's more to come.

ENCHANTED KITCHEN CLEANERS

Working with natural cleaning agents is a great way to enhance the vibrational frequency of your kitchen.

Start with base ingredients like vinegar, baking soda, and sodium borate (also known as "borax") and add the power of essential botanical oils to create fresh, pleasing scents and an extra boost of magical energy. If you like, you can tailor the recipes below to create a specific type of energetic enhancement for your kitchen.

For extra magical "oomph," charge the ingredients with your intention before mixing them together.

Physical and magical properties of essential oils used in natural cleaners

Bergamot: anti-bacterial, positive energy, confidence, success, peace and harmony
Eucalyptus: anti-bacterial, protection, fresh energy
Lemon: positive energy, purification
Lavender: anti-bacterial, purification, peace and harmony
Juniper: purification, protection, healing
Peppermint: anti-bacterial purification (also repels insects and mice)

Rosemary: anti-bacterial, purification, protection
Ylang ylang: positive energy, peace and harmony

ALL-PURPOSE KITCHEN SURFACE CLEANER

Spray down tables, countertops, stove tops, etc. with this effective and delightfully scented concoction. Then just wipe with a cloth, allow the surface to dry, and you're done!

You will need:

- ½ cup white vinegar
- 1 tablespoon water
- 4 drops lemon oil
- 3 drops lavender oil
- 2 drops juniper oil
- 1 drop peppermint oil
- 2 tablespoons baking soda
- Clean spray bottle

Instructions:

Add the vinegar, water and essential oils to the spray bottle and swish the ingredients together to blend.

Then add the baking soda, fill the bottle to the top with water and shake gently.

NATURAL OVEN CLEANER

While this solution may not be quite enough to tackle a long-neglected oven, it should do the trick once you've given your oven a thorough deep clean with a conventional cleaner. For best results, wipe off any encrusted grease or food remnants with newspaper before applying the mixture.

You will need:

- 2 cups hot water
- 1 tablespoon natural, chemical-free dish soap
- 1 teaspoon borax
- 3 drops lemon oil
- 2 drops eucalyptus oil
- Clean spray bottle

Instructions:

Spray liberally inside the oven and let sit for 20 minutes.

Wipe off with a clean cloth.

TABLES OF CORRESPONDENCE FOR THE KITCHEN WITCH

Here, you will find four tables of correspondence you may find useful. Remember, you should always trust your intuition when selecting ingredients. As you become more experienced, much of this will become second nature. For newer kitchen witches, though, these tables can be used as solid foundations in your new practice.

CULINARY HERBS

Herb	General Magical Uses
Basil	Fosters loving vibrations, protection, wards off negativities in a home
Bay Leaf	Protection, purification, healing, strength, good fortune, money, and success
Cinnamon	Love, luck, prosperity, success, raises spiritual vibrations
Dandelion (fresh leaves)	Divination, interaction with the spirit world, wishes
Nutmeg	Money, prosperity, good luck, protection
Oregano	Peace, deepening love relationships, releasing old relationships
Parsley	Protection, money, luck, lust, strength, vitality
Rosemary	Love and lust spells, promotes healthy rest
Sage	Longevity, wisdom, protection, dispels negative energy
Star Anise	Luck, spiritual connection, psychic and magical power
Thyme	Attracts loyalty, affection, psychic abilities

MAGICAL USES FOR FOODS ACCORDING TO COLOR

Color	Magical Attributes	Used in Magic for	Example Foods
Red	Passion, courage, strength, intense emotions	Love, physical energy, health, willpower	Apples, tomatoes, peppers, cherries, strawberries
Orange	Energy, attraction, vitality, stimulation	Adaptability to sudden changes, encouragement, power	Squash, pumpkin, cantaloupe, carrots
Yellow	Intellect, inspiration, imagination, knowledge	Communication, confidence, divination, study	Lemons, corn, golden beets, bananas
Green	Abundance, growth, wealth, renewal, balance	Prosperity, employment, fertility, health, good luck	Avocados, peppers, kale, lettuce, chard, zucchini, broccoli
Blue	Peace, truth, wisdom, protection, patience	Healing, psychic ability, harmony in the home, understanding	Blueberries, blue corn, purple potatoes (turn blue when cooked)

Color	Magical Attributes	Used in Magic for	Example Foods
Violet	Spirituality, wisdom, devotion, peace, idealism	Divination, enhancing nurturing qualities, balancing sensitivity	Eggplant, purple carrots, purple cabbage, plums
White	Peace, innocence, illumination, purity	Cleansing, clarity, establishing order, spiritual growth and understanding	Onions, mushrooms, rice, yoghurts, all milks
Black	Dignity, force, stability, protection	Banishing and releasing negative energies, transformation, enlightenment	Black beans, blackberries, chia seeds, rice
Brown	Endurance, solidity, grounding, strength	Balance, concentration, material gain, home, companion animals	Lentils, rice, wheat, grains, dark chocolate
Pink	Affection, friendship, companionship, spiritual healing	Romance, spiritual awakening, partnerships, children's magic	Beets, rhubarb, ginger (when pickled), raspberries

PANTRY STAPLES AND MAGICAL GOALS

Food Item	Magical Goals
Bread	Abundance, health, security, kinship
Beans	Luck, money, divination, decision-making
Butter	Spirituality, peace, relationships
Cheese	Moon magic, joy, health, completion of goals
Eggs	Fertility, mysticism, Goddess magic
Honey	Health, happiness, love, lust, sex, purification, wisdom, stability
Milk	Love, spirituality, sustenance, motherhood
Rice	Money, fertility, protection, good luck
Salt	Protection, grounding, purification
Sugar	Love, affection, banishing gossip
Vinegar	Purification, protection, cleansing (white vinegar)

THE ELEMENTS IN THE KITCHEN

Element	Magical Energies	Tools	Example Foods
Earth	Stability, discipline, prosperity, abundance	Plates, spoons, baking pans, cutting board	Grains, flour, root vegetables, cheeses, maple syrup, peanuts
Air	Intellect, communication, imagination, harmony	Forks, knives, blender, oven fan	Honey, bamboo shoots, rice, bananas, dandelions, corn
Fire	Passion, illumination, transformation, enthusiasm	Skillet, oven, oven burners, grill, toaster	Hot peppers, salsa, basil, radishes, sunflower seeds
Water	Emotion, sensitivity, intuition, empathy	Cups, bowls, pots, sink, dishwater	All beverages, lemons, lettuce, cucumbers, plums
Spirit	All	All	All

CONCLUSION

Cooking and magic have quite a lot in common. Both involve the use of various ingredients and natural forces to create something new, and both are undertaken to improve the well-being of the practitioner. Most delightfully, both cooking and magic also present infinite possibilities—so much so that even the most experienced chefs and magicians can still learn new tricks, techniques, and ingredients no matter how many years they've been practicing.

Hopefully, you've learned enough from this beginner's guide to inspire you to keep reading more about the endless ways in which you can combine the art of cooking with the art of magic. To get you on your way, you'll find a list of further resources to consult on the following page. As always, listen to your inner voice as you navigate new information. And remember to give yourself time to experiment with new recipes and techniques. You will learn much from both your successes and your mistakes (we all do make mistakes, after all!).

May the magical energies of the Earth's infinite abundance be with you on your journey!

SUGGESTIONS FOR FURTHER READING

Books regarding kitchen magic can take many different approaches. Some are cookbooks in their own right, consisting mostly of recipes, while others focus more on providing general information, tips and kitchen-related spellwork (such as this guide). The resources listed below may fit either (or both) of these categories, but those with a heavy emphasis on recipes will be marked with an asterisk (*).

As with all things related to Wicca and Paganism, you may find conflicting information regarding magical correspondences, techniques, and other topics within these books. Think of these resources as jumping-off points toward your own exploration and discoveries in the realm of kitchen witchery—ultimately, experience will be your best teacher. Happy reading (and cooking)!

Scott Cunningham, *Cunningham's Encyclopedia of Wicca in the Kitchen* (1990)

Barbara Ann Daca, *One Pot Witchery-Stone Soup: The Hidden Grimoire Of The Kitchen Hedge Witch* (2008)*

Anna Franklin, *The Hearth Witch's Compendium: Magical and Natural Living for Every Day* (2017)

Cerridwen Greenleaf, *The Book of Kitchen Witchery: Spells, Recipes, and Rituals for Magical Meals, an Enchanted Garden, and a Happy Home* (2016)

Cait Johnson, *Witch in the Kitchen: Magical Cooking for All Seasons* (2001)*

Rachel Patterson, *Grimoire of a Kitchen Witch: An Essential Guide to Witchcraft* (2013)

Patricia Telesco, *A Kitchen Witch's Cookbook* (1994)*

Soraya, *The Kitchen Witch: A Year-round Witch's Brew of Seasonal Recipes, Lotions and Potions for Every Pagan Festival* (2011)*

Leandra Witchwood, *Magick in the Kitchen: A Real-World Spiritual Guide for Manifesting the Kitchen Witch Within* (2015)

Jamie Wood and Tara Seefeldt, *The Wicca Cookbook, Second Edition: Recipes, Ritual, and Lore* (2000)*

DID YOU ENJOY *WICCA KITCHEN WITCHERY?*

Again let me thank you for purchasing and reading my guide. There are a number of great books on the topic, so I really appreciate you choosing my guide.

If you enjoyed the book, I'd like to ask for a small favor in return. If possible, I'd love for you to take a couple of minutes to leave a review for this book on Amazon.

Your feedback will help me to make improvements to this guide, as well as writing books on other topics that might be of interest to you. Hopefully this will allow me to create even better guides in future!

OTHER BOOKS BY LISA CHAMBERLAIN

Wicca for Beginners: A Guide to Wiccan Beliefs, Rituals, Magic, and Witchcraft

Wicca Herbal Magic: A Beginner's Guide to Practicing Wiccan Herbal Magic, with Simple Herb Spells

Wicca Book of Spells: A Book of Shadows for Wiccans, Witches, and Other Practitioners of Magic

Wicca Book of Herbal Spells: A Book of Shadows for Wiccans, Witches, and Other Practitioners of Herbal Magic

Wicca Candle Magic: A Beginner's Guide to Practicing Wiccan Candle Magic, with Simple Candle Spells

Wicca Crystal Magic: A Beginner's Guide to Practicing Wiccan Crystal Magic, with Simple Crystal Spells

Wicca Kitchen Witchery: A Beginner's Guide to Magical Cooking, with Simple Spells and Recipes

Wicca Moon Magic: A Wiccan's Guide and Grimoire for Working Magic with Lunar Energies

Wicca Essential Oils Magic: A Beginner's Guide to Working with Magical Oils, with Simple Recipes and Spells

Wicca Elemental Magic: A Guide to the Elements, Witchcraft, and Magical Spells

Tarot for Beginners: A Guide to Psychic Tarot Reading, Real Tarot Card Meanings, and Simple Tarot Spreads

Wicca Magical Deities: A Guide to the Wiccan God and Goddess, and Choosing a Deity to Work Magic With

Wicca Wheel of the Year Magic: A Beginner's Guide to the Sabbats, with History, Symbolism, Celebration Ideas, and Dedicated Sabbat Spells

Wicca Living a Magical Life: A Guide to Initiation and Navigating Your Journey in the Craft

Magic and the Law of Attraction: A Witch's Guide to the Magic of Intention, Raising Your Frequency, and Building Your Reality

Wicca Altar and Tools: A Beginner's Guide to Wiccan Altars, Tools for Spellwork, and Casting the Circle

Wicca Finding Your Path: A Beginner's Guide to Wiccan Traditions, Solitary Practitioners, Eclectic Witches, Covens, and Circles

Wicca Book of Shadows: A Beginner's Guide to Keeping Your Own Book of Shadows and the History of Grimoires

Modern Witchcraft and Magic for Beginners: A Guide to Traditional and Contemporary Paths, with Magical Techniques for the Beginner Witch

FREE GIFT REMINDER

I'd hate for you to miss out, so here is one final reminder of the free, downloadable eBook that I'm giving away to my readers.

Wicca: Little Book of Wiccan Spells is ideal for any Wiccans who want to start practicing magic. It contains a collection of ten spells that I have deemed suitable for beginners.

You can download it by visiting:

www.wiccaliving.com/bonus

I hope you enjoy it.

26854897R00072

Printed in Great Britain
by Amazon